P9-EDX-042

RAY METHODS OF HEALING

Zachary F. Lansdowne, Ph.D.

RAY
M E T H O D S
OF
HEALING

SAMUEL WEISER, INC.

York Beach, Maine

First published in 1993 by
Samuel Weiser, Inc.
Box 612
York Beach, ME 03910

Copyright © 1993 Zachary F. Lansdowne

All rights reserved. No part of this publication may be repro-
duced or transmitted in any form or by any means, electronic
or mechanical, including photocopy, without permission in
writing from the publisher. Reviewers may quote brief passages.

Library of Congress Cataloging-in-Publication Data

Lansdowne, Zachary F.
    Ray methods of healing / by Zachary Lansdowne.
        p.   cm.
    Includes bibliographical references and index.
    1. Seven rays (Occultism)—Therapeutic use.   I. Title,
RZ999.L26   1993
615.8'51—dc20   92-45541
                                                              CIP

ISBN 0-87728-745-7
BJ

Cover art copyright © 1993 Ananda Kurt Pilz.
Used by kind permission of the Walter Holl Agency, Germany.

Typeset in 11 point Baskerville

Printed in the United States of America

The paper used in this publication meets the minimum requirements of the American National Standard for Permanence of
Paper for Printed Library Materials Z39.48-1984.

CONTENTS

List of Tables

Acknowledgments

Appreciation is expressed to William L. Kovacs, Donna Mitchell-Moniak, and Maurice A. E. Rothman for their careful and thoughtful comments on an earlier version of this book. Appreciation is also expressed to the Lucis Publishing Company for permission to quote from the various books by Alice A. Bailey.

Chapter 1

━━━━✳━━━━

INTRODUCTION

It is only with the heart that one can see rightly;
what is essential is invisible to the eye.
—Antoine de Saint-Exupéry

In a book published in 1953, Alice A. Bailey presented seven symbolic formulas of healing but with virtually no explanation. Our purpose here is to clarify those formulas and give a complete explanation, showing that each formula can be interpreted in three ways. One interpretation describes how perceptible forms can be used in a *method of exoteric healing,* such as counseling, education, homeopathy, or the therapeutic application of gemstones. Another interpretation describes how soul qualities can be used in a *method of service,* such as raja yoga or white magic. And the third interpretation describes how subtle energies can be used in a *method of esoteric healing,* such as radiatory healing or pranic healing.

Although Bailey did not explain the actual meanings of her formulas of healing, she did give some intriguing information about their past, present, and future. Concerning their past, she wrote that these formulas had an ancient origin and were "gathered out of the *Book of Rules for Initiated Disciples.*" Concerning the time that they were published, she wrote that her purpose was to "lay the foundation for a future structure of knowledge" and to generate "a wise and searching expectancy." She also wrote that these symbolic formulas were "susceptible of three significances, the lowest of which the modern student may succeed in interpreting for himself if he reflects adequately and lives spiritually." And with regard to their future, she predicted that "some disciple in the early part of next century will take these techniques or magical statements, relating to the healing work, and interpret them and elucidate them."[1]

The Human Constitution

Although Bailey's healing formulas are written in a concise way, they include symbols that integrate and synthesize a vast amount of philosophical information. So that our interpretations of these symbols can be understood, we shall briefly review the following basic concepts from theosophy: the seven planes, human constitution, and initiations.

According to theosophy, the solar system is sevenfold in its construction. Although only the physical world can be perceived with ordinary human senses, it is claimed that there are also six higher worlds of progressively subtler matter that interpenetrate the physical. These worlds are called *planes,* and their names are commonly listed as follows: adi, monadic, atmic, buddhic, mental, emotional, and physical. The adi is the first or highest plane, and the physical is the seventh or lowest plane.

As shown in figure 1, each plane has seven subplanes. For instance, the physical plane consists of the following subplanes: first ether, second ether, third ether, fourth ether, gaseous, liquid, and solid. The three lowest subplanes—gaseous, liquid, and solid—comprise the dense world of mat-

---

[1] A. A. Bailey, *Esoteric Healing* (1953; reprint; New York: Lucis Publishing Company, 1977), pp. 694, 705, 706.

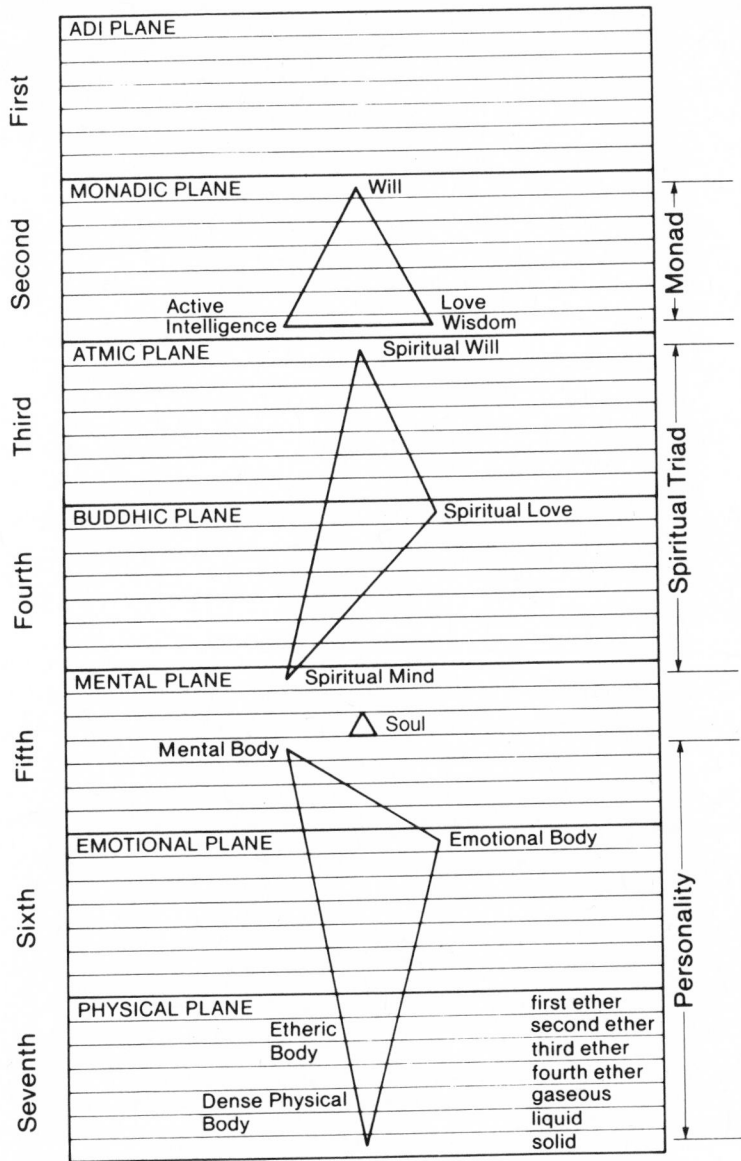

Figure 1. Inner Human Constitution.

ter and are perceptible with ordinary human senses. The four highest subplanes represent the etheric region. Although imperceptible with ordinary senses, these four ethers are considered to be part of the physical realm.

A human being is said to have a "vehicle of consciousness" or a "body" on all of the planes. These bodies are organized into four main groups or clusters: monad, spiritual triad, soul, and personality. Figure 1 (on page 3) shows the relationships between these clusters and the seven planes. Next, we shall discuss each cluster separately.

The real self of a human being is the *monad,* sometimes called the spirit. It is a unit of consciousness, a spark of the Supreme Fire, the innermost source of existence, and the wellspring of human life. The monad resides on the second or monadic plane but the roots of its life are in the first or adi plane. Because the first two planes represent the unmanifest world, the monad is a point of absolute abstraction, subjectivity, and latency. As illustrated in the figure, the monad possesses three qualities: will, love-wisdom, and active intelligence.

The word *reflection* is used when a force existing on a higher plane passes down to a lower level where it is affected by a denser kind of matter. The *spiritual triad* is a reflection of the monad and is the channel through which the monad functions in the field of manifestation. The spiritual triad consists of the spiritual will, spiritual love, and spiritual mind. The spiritual will expresses the will of the monad. It resides on the third or atmic plane and is sometimes called the "will-to-good." When evoked, the spiritual will becomes an immanent, propulsive, clarifying, and driving force concerned with cooperating with the divine plan and establishing right human relationships. The spiritual love expresses the love-wisdom of the monad and resides on the fourth or buddhic plane. When evoked, it allows the divine germ to be sensed in all bodily forms and enables the essential unity of all human beings to be perceived. The spiritual mind expresses the active intelligence of the monad. It occupies the highest mental subplane and is sometimes called the "higher abstract mind." When evoked, the spiritual mind provides intuitive insights that are clear and direct perceptions of truth.

The *soul*—sometimes called the causal body or egoic lotus—also resides on the mental plane. Because the soul is the storehouse for the abstracted essence, or wisdom, gained from a person's experience, it gradually evolves over time. The soul of an undeveloped person uses matter from only the third mental subplane (counting from the top), which is illustrated in figure 1 (on page 3). But with development, the soul also uses matter from the second subplane, enabling it to extend over both the second and third subplanes. Because the soul is the vehicle for abstract thought, an undeveloped person is capable of only a limited amount of such thinking. But a developed person, whose soul is using higher matter, is capable of profound thought having loftiness, subtlety, and wisdom. The soul of a developed person also acts as an intermediary and conveys intuitions from the spiritual triad to the personality.

The *personality* has four parts. The mental body—sometimes called the concrete mind or simply the mind—is the highest part and occupies the four lowest subplanes of the mental plane. It is the vehicle for concrete thought and gives the power of discrimination. The emotional or astral body spans all seven subplanes of the emotional plane, and it gives the capacity to sense, desire, aspire, and attract. The etheric or vital body occupies the four highest subplanes of the physical plane, which is the etheric region, and it gives the power to act and be energetic. Finally, the dense physical body, located on the three lowest subplanes of the physical plane, enables activity to take place in the objective, tangible world.

A human being is essentially the monad (or spirit), reflecting as the spiritual triad in the field of manifestation, demonstrating through the gradually evolving soul, and using the personality to contact the three lowest planes for the purpose of gaining experience. We learn to integrate these various parts gradually and progressively. Prior to reaching the spiritual path, we learn to integrate the physical body with the emotional body, these two with the mental body, and then these three with the personality as a whole.

According to theosophy, the spiritual path consists of several distinct segments. The first segment is called the path of probation. We start to travel on this segment when we are aware of an inner conflict between personality and soul, and we become willing to be taught by the soul. When our outer behavior is guided by the wisdom of the soul, we reach the end of the path of probation and experience an expansion of consciousness called the first initiation. The second segment is the path of discipleship, and it extends from the first initiation to another expansion of consciousness called the third initiation. The goal on this path is to complete the integration of the personality with the soul. The third segment is the path of initiation, and it extends from the third initiation to even higher initiations. The goal here is to integrate the soul-infused personality with the spiritual triad, and then with the monad.

Invocation is the act of calling for help from a factor that is greater, more inclusive, and more enlightened. Evocation is the response of the greater factor. The integrations on the spiritual path occur through a process of invocation and evocation. In each case, the parts of the human constitution that have already been integrated invoke the next higher part, and then that higher part responds according to the degree of understanding and dynamic tension displayed by the lower integrated parts. The effort of the lower parts is invocation, and the success of the invocatory rite is evocation. For instance, an aspirant progresses on the path of probation by creating a point of invocatory tension in the personality, which then evokes a response from the soul.

The Seven Rays

Bailey's symbolic formulas are closely related to the typology of the seven rays. Because the *ray* of something refers to its essential quality, the seven rays provide a way of classifying various phenomena in terms of their essential qualities. The seven rays fall into two different groups. The first three rays are the major rays. The last four rays are the minor rays and can be produced by the interplay of the major ones. As an analogy, the visible spectrum consists of seven different colors; three colors are primary and can be blended to produce the other four colors.

Helena P. Blavatsky, the founder of the Theosophical Society, presented the concept of the seven rays in her celebrated book *The Secret Doctrine*, which was originally published in 1888. Blavatsky also cited references to the seven rays, which she found within ancient sources including the Hindu Rig Veda, Hermetic philosophy, Gnostic texts, the Jewish Cabala, and the Christian Bible. But she did not differentiate between the ray types nor show how they could be applied in a practical way.[2]

During the last one hundred years, a number of other writers have expanded or elaborated the teachings on the seven rays. Charles W. Leadbeater gave a differentiating quality and an affirmation for each of the seven rays.[3] Ernest Wood wrote the first book specifically devoted to the seven rays and described the personal characteristics of people who display each ray.[4] Alice A. Bailey made an important contribution with the publication of her five-volume *Treatise on the Seven Rays*, which discusses the application of this typology to psychology, astrology, healing, and initiation.[5] Geoffrey Hodson summa-

---

[2] H. P. Blavatsky, *The Secret Doctrine* (1888; reprint; Pasadena, CA: Theosophical University Press, 1977).

[3] C. W. Leadbeater, *The Science of the Sacraments* (Adyar, Madras, India: Theosophical Publishing House, 1920).

[4] E. Wood, *The Seven Rays* (1925; reprint; Wheaton, IL: Theosophical Publishing House, 1984).

[5] A. A. Bailey, *A Treatise on the Seven Rays*, in 5 volumes: *Esoteric Psychology*, vol. 1 (1936; reprint; New York: Lucis Publishing Company, 1975); *Esoteric Psychology*, vol. 2 (1942; reprint; New York: Lucis Publishing Company, 1975); *Esoteric Astrology* (1951; reprint; New York: Lucis Publishing Company, 1977); *Esoteric Healing* (1953; reprint; New York: Lucis Publishing Company, 1977); and *The Rays and the Initiations* (1960; reprint; New York: Lucis Publishing Company, 1976).

rized the characteristics of people who are predominantly influenced by each ray, including their basic qualities, associated occupations, greatest good and evil, sources of suffering, quest and driving impulse, methods of teaching and achievement, weaknesses, and highest attainment.[6] Roberto Assagioli described the key developmental tasks for people of each ray type and showed how this typology could be applied within the branch of psychology or counseling known as psychosynthesis.[7] Michael Robbins developed tools, including a self-administered and computer-scored test, that could help counselors to assess the predominant rays of their clients.[8] Robert Gerard's survey article provides a helpful commentary and perspective concerning the foregoing contributions as well as others that have been made.[9]

Most of the earlier books on the seven rays apply this typology to psychology. These books show that each element of the human constitution has a predominant ray that can vary from person to person. Thus, one way to characterize the nature of a given human being is to specify the rays of that person's physical body, emotional body, mental body, personality, soul, and so forth. The apparent quality of the person is generally the ray of the highest factor that he or she expresses. If the person makes further progress and expresses a yet higher factor, then the earlier ray becomes the subray of the new controlling ray. For instance, as one learns to integrate the personality, the ray of the personality becomes the dominating quality. But as one learns to integrate the personality with the soul, the soul ray becomes the dominating quality, and the personality ray becomes the subray of the soul ray.

---

[6] G. Hodson, *The Seven Human Temperaments* (1952; reprint; Adyar, Madras, India: Theosophical Publishing House, 1984).

[7] R. Assagioli, M.D., *Psychosynthesis Typology* (London: Institute of Psychosynthesis, 1983).

[8] M. D. Robbins, Ph.D., *Tapestry of the Gods* (Jersey City Heights, NJ: University of the Seven Rays Publishing House, 1988).

[9] R. Gerard, Ph.D., "Commentary," in *Tapestry of the Gods*, pp. v-xxii.

Because each of Bailey's symbolic formulas of healing corresponds to one of the seven rays, the present book applies this typology to healing. The next three chapters interpret each formula as describing three methods of healing (exoteric, service, and esoteric) including the key principles, the healer's preparation, how the healing force is applied, and the effects on the patient. Any method of healing can be thought of as an outer form that expresses an inner quality. The three healing methods that are provided by any one of the seven formulas express the ray (or quality) associated with that formula, although the methods have different forms. Each chapter uses the seven rays to classify the highest influences that are expressed through the healing methods of that chapter. Because the influences are higher in each successive chapter, the earlier rays are treated as the subrays of the new controlling influence, as explained next.

Chapter 2, which presents seven methods of exoteric healing, views the soul of every human being as having seven different qualities that correspond to the seven rays. In the method of exoteric healing given for a particular ray, the healer is considered as being centered primarily in the personality while being able to evoke the corresponding quality from the soul. None of the methods requires that the healer has an attainment greater than the first initiation.

Chapter 3, which describes seven methods of service, views the souls of all human beings as falling into seven different categories that correspond to the seven rays. The predominant quality of a given person's soul—called the soul ray—determines that person's method of working on the spiritual path and eventual destiny. The seven qualities of the soul, referred to in chapter 2, are treated as the seven subrays of the soul ray. In the method of service described for a particular ray, the healer becomes centered temporarily in the soul and gains the ability to express outwardly the various characteristics of the corresponding soul ray. None of the methods requires the healer's attainment to be greater than the second initiation.

Chapter 4, which describes seven methods of esoteric healing, views the monad of every human being as having three qualities that correspond to the three major rays. In each method of esoteric healing, the healer must first become centered in the soul and then evoke one of the three monadic qualities. The healer still can express the seven types of soul qualities referred to in chapter 2, but each type becomes the vehicle for displaying the overshadowing monadic quality. In other words, the seven qualities of the soul become the seven subrays of the monadic quality. Thus, the role of the monadic quality in chapter 4 is similar to that of the soul ray in chapter 3. In the method of esoteric healing given for each of the three major rays, the healer must evoke the corresponding monadic quality. And in the method given for each of the four minor rays, the healer must express the corresponding subray of one of the monadic qualities. None of the methods requires the healer's attainment to be greater than the third initiation.

Consequently, Bailey's healing formulas are extraordinary. They yield both instruction in the art of healing and a way of organizing the full spectrum of therapeutic techniques, revealing their inherent horizonal and vertical relationships. The end result is a comprehensive philosophy of healing.

Chapter 2

---※---

METHODS OF EXOTERIC HEALING

I will keep pure and holy both my life and my art.
—Hippocrates

Exoteric refers to the external or outside world and therefore to what is readily perceivable through the five physical senses. A method of exoteric healing delivers the healing energy through perceptible instruments or forms, such as physical behavior, spoken words, teaching materials, sounds, colors, books, medicines, or gemstones. Bailey published a symbolic formula of healing for each of the seven rays, and we shall interpret those formulas as describing methods of exoteric healing. The fundamental premise is that the soul of any human being has seven different qualities that correspond to the seven rays. Each method of exoteric healing assumes that the healer is polarized or centered primarily in the personality while being able to evoke the associated quality from the soul.

Healing means bringing harmony or normality to different parts of the same organism or living structure. The methods of exoteric healing described in this chapter are based on different concepts of what constitutes an organism, and some methods are based on multiple concepts. The fourth-, sixth-, and seventh-ray methods are concerned with physical healing and bring harmony to the various organs of the physical body. The third-, fourth-, and fifth-ray methods are concerned with psychological healing and help to integrate the various elements of the personality. The first-, second-, and fifth-ray methods help to integrate the personality with the soul. And the fourth-ray method also helps to unify a group of human beings so that they can function together in a harmonious way.

In this chapter, each ray is prefaced by Bailey's symbolic formula. The interpretations that follow, as well as those in chapters 3 and 4, are solely the responsibility of the present writer and may not be what were originally intended. Consequently, the reader must carefully judge the accuracy of what follows.

Ray One

Let the dynamic force which rules the hearts of all within Shamballa come to my aid, for I am worthy of that aid. Let it descend unto the third, pass to the fifth and focus on the seventh. These words mean not what doth at sight appear. The third, the fifth, the seventh lie within the first and come from out the Central Sun of spiritual livingness. The highest then awakens within the one who knows and within the one who must be healed and thus the two are one. This is mystery deep. The blending of the healing force effects the work desired; it may bring death, that great release, and re-establish thus the fifth, the third, the first, but not the seventh.[1]

The first ray is called the ray of will or power. In the method of exoteric healing described by the first formula, the

---

[1] A. A. Bailey, *Esoteric Healing* (1953; reprint; New York: Lucis Publishing Company, 1978), pp. 706, 707.

healer invokes the will of the soul and then lives a life that is an influential example to others. Because this life is one of service, we shall refer to the healer as the server.

The first sentence of the formula refers to *Shamballa*. In Tibetan Buddhism, Shamballa is the name of a mythological kingdom that is said to lie hidden behind unexplored snow peaks somewhere north of Tibet. The stories about Shamballa probably inspired James Hilton to write the novel *Lost Horizon*, in which he described an earthly paradise called Shangri-La that is also hidden behind snow peaks in the Tibetan area.[2] The earliest known references to Shamballa occur in books written in the Tibetan language around the 11th century A.D., but these are believed to be translations of older works written in Sanskrit. In fact, the name *Shamballa* is a Sanskrit word that can be translated as "the source of happiness."

According to the Tibetan myths, Shamballa has flowering parks, golden-roofed pagodas, and jeweled palaces. The inhabitants live in peace and harmony, free of sickness, and their crops never fail. They speak the language of Sanskrit and study various sciences including medicine, astronomy, and psychology. Although the inhabitants are spiritually advanced, they are not fully enlightened but still retain some human failings and illusions. Because of their focus on attaining enlightenment, they devote most of their time to the study and practice of the highest wisdom known to Tibetan Buddhism, which is called the Kalacakra or "Wheel of Time." This teaching shows how to find eternity in the passing moment, the indestructible in the midst of destruction. Rather than renouncing worldly activities for the asceticism of a hermit or monk, the people of Shamballa use everything, including the distractions of luxury and family life, for a spiritual purpose. In theosophical terminology, they have become soul-infused personalities, which means that their personalities are ruled by the will of their souls.[3]

---

[2] J. Hilton, *Lost Horizon* (1933; reprint; New York: Pocket Books, 1990).

[3] E. Bernbaum, Ph.D., *The Way to Shambhala* (1980; reprint; Los Angeles: Jeremy P. Tarcher, 1989), pp. 5-12.

As stated earlier, this chapter discusses the soul's seven qualities that correspond to the seven rays. The first-ray quality of the soul is the will, and it is sometimes called the *goodwill*. When evoked, goodwill is experienced as the urge to serve others. This urge to serve is an instinctive and innate impetus of the soul, just as the urges of self-preservation and reproduction are instinctive and innate drives of the physical body. Goodwill is a creative impetus because it can produce tangible results on the physical plane. When goodwill begins to dominate the personality, the first effect is the demonstration of a real understanding and true helpfulness for one's immediate family and group. As goodwill becomes stronger through use, the effect spreads out from the small surrounding family group to the neighborhood, until eventually the influence becomes nationwide and then worldwide.[4]

Before one can become an influential example for other people, one has to prepare oneself. As described in the first sentence of the formula, the server must invoke the first-ray quality of the soul, the goodwill, which is the purpose or motive that rules the lives of all within the mythical kingdom of Shamballa ("Let the dynamic force which rules the hearts of all within Shamballa come to my aid"). For this invocation to be successful, the server must have already accomplished several preliminary steps ("for I am worthy of that aid"): transmuting the desire for worldly accomplishments into the aspiration of being an instrument for the soul, and using the mental body to coordinate or integrate the energies of the personality.

The second sentence of the formula gives the steps that are needed for manifesting the purpose of the soul. The first step is creating a mental plan for solving some problem or meeting some need. For instance, the plan might be to establish or help with welfare movements, philanthropic endeavors, educational improvements, or hospices. Creating such a plan

---

[4] A. A. Bailey, *Esoteric Psychology,* vol. 2 (1942; reprint; New York: Lucis Publishing Company, 1981), pp. 125-128.

involves using the third-ray quality of the soul, which is active intelligence or adaptability. So that goodwill is expressed through the mental body, the first-ray quality must guide and control the application of the third-ray quality ("Let it descend unto the third").

Before implementing the mental plan, one should stop and observe one's emotional responses. *Glamour* can be defined as being an emotional reaction that prevents clear perception. If a particular glamour is seen, such as self-pity, pride, or self-justification, the next step is using the mind to investigate that glamour. As discussed in more detail in the sixth-ray section of chapter 3, eradication of a glamour requires discovering the underlying beliefs and then inquiring into their truth or falsehood. This effort of discovery and inquiry involves applying the fifth-ray quality of the soul, because that is the ray of scientific investigation. So that goodwill is expressed through the emotional body, the first-ray quality must guide and control the application of the fifth-ray quality ("pass to the fifth").

After creating a mental plan and eliminating any glamours, one can take the final step: engaging in appropriate physical activities so that the plan manifests in the form of tangible service. Manifestation is a seventh-ray activity, because that is the ray of ceremonial order or magic. In order for goodwill to be expressed through physical behavior, the first-ray quality of the soul must guide and control the application of the seventh-ray quality ("and focus on the seventh").

Although the preceding paragraphs seem to suggest that the first-ray quality is different from the third-, fifth-, and seventh-ray qualities, this difference is an illusion ("These words mean not what doth at sight appear"). The first-ray quality is able to control those other ray qualities only because of the following circumstance: subrays corresponding to each of those other rays lie within the first-ray quality and are part of the goodwill coming out from the soul ("The third, the fifth, the seventh lie within the first and come from out the Central Sun of spiritual livingness"). For instance, the third subray of the first-ray quality has the power to guide and control the appli-

Table 1. The Major Etheric Chakras.*

English Name	Sanskrit Name	Approximate Location	Number of Petals
Head or Crown	Sahasrara	Top of head	Inner circle of 12 major petals surrounded by an outer circle of 960 secondary petals
Brow	Ajna	Between the eyebrows, in front of head	2 primary petals, each of which is divided into 48 smaller petals, resulting in 96 petals altogether
Throat	Vishuddha	Back of neck	16 petals
Heart	Anahata	Between shoulder blades	12 petals
Solar plexus	Manipura	Behind stomach	10 petals
Sacral	Svadhisthana	Lower part of lumbar area	6 petals
Basic	Muladhara	Base of spine	4 petals

*Sources: A. A. Bailey, *The Soul and Its Mechanism* (1930; reprint; New York: Lucis Publishing Company, 1976), p. 111; A. A. Bailey, *Letters on Occult Meditation* (1922; reprint; New York: Lucis Publishing Company, 1974), pp. 77, 78; and A. A. Bailey, *A Treatise on White Magic* (1934; reprint; New York: Lucis Publishing Company, 1974), pp. 190, 199.

cation of the third-ray quality. In other words, when the general purpose of serving others is expressed through the narrower purpose of constructing an appropriate plan, then that narrower purpose can guide and control the mental effort of constructing the plan.

Through the application of the foregoing steps, goodwill awakens within all levels of the server's personality and manifests outwardly as effective, impersonal service ("The highest then awakens within the one who knows"). If the onlookers have the proper degree of readiness, they will be inspired by the example of the server and thus will proceed to do likewise ("and within the one who must be healed and thus the two are one"). To have this readiness, the onlookers must have the capacity to hear the intuitive voice of their own souls, enabling them to recognize the server's example as being the outer symbol or confirmation of what they already know deep within themselves but have doubted or ignored ("This is mystery deep").

The enumeration in the last sentence refers to the chakras. The word *chakra* means "wheel" in Sanskrit, and it refers to a subtle wheel of energy in the etheric body that vitalizes a portion of the dense physical body. The etheric body contains seven major chakras and twenty-one minor chakras. For each major chakra, Table 1 lists the English name, traditional Sanskrit name, and approximate location. A major chakra is sometimes symbolized as a lotus consisting of a specific number of petals, and this number is also given in Table 1. Because each petal represents a particular type of force, the number of petals associated with a given chakra indicates the number of different forces that can be expressed by that chakra.

The blending of the server's example with the intuitive voice within each onlooker performs the healing work ("The blending of the healing force effects the work desired"). The blending may induce the onlookers to sacrifice the self-centered ambitions of the personality ("it may bring death"), which releases the inner power of the soul ("that great release"). In this case, the onlookers will repeat the same process that the server used during the previously described stage of preparation ("and re-establish thus"). Specifically, they will transmute the desire of the fifth or solar plexus chakra into aspiration; employ the third or throat chakra to coordinate the personality; and then invoke the goodwill, which is registered by the first or crown chakra ("the fifth, the third, the first"). Releasing the power of the soul does not require the development or activation of the seventh or basic chakra ("but not the seventh"), although such activation is needed for a later stage on the spiritual path.

This first method of healing helps to reorient the personality, and it is a method that is especially appropriate for rescuing troubled adolescents. When parents are weak, violent, absent, or misguided, teenagers are often tempted to evoke their imagination and ambition along false and wrong lines, leading to delinquency, drug abuse, and crime. Bailey's formula shows how these adolescents could be helped by encountering positive role models, perhaps as part of public schools, drug treatment programs, church or Boy Scout activities, or programs that assign mentors. The most influential exponents of a higher way of living are people who have pulled themselves up from circumstances similar to what the teenagers are facing. Through the examples of their own lives, the positive role models show that there is a choice that everyone must make between lower and higher values and that those who choose the higher values will escape from many of the problems and miseries of daily life.

Ray Two

Let the healing energy descend, carrying its dual lines of life and its magnetic force. Let that magnetic living force withdraw and supplement that which is present in the seventh, opposing four and six to three and seven, but dealing not with five. The circular, inclusive vortex—descending to the point—disturbs, removes and then supplies and thus the work is done.

The heart revolves; two hearts revolve as one; the twelve within the vehicle, the twelve within the head and the twelve upon the plane of soul endeavor, cooperate as one and thus the work is done. Two energies achieve this consummation and the three whose number is a twelve respond to the greater twelve. The life is known and the years prolonged.[5]

The name of the second ray is love-wisdom. The second-ray formula shows how the qualities of love and wisdom can be expressed through counseling, and it covers four aspects of a counseling session: invocation, content, process, and participants. We shall refer to the healer as the counselor and the recipient as the aspirant.

At the beginning of a session, the counselor invokes greater understanding from the soul and helps the aspirant to make the same invocation ("Let the healing energy descend"). For instance, the counselor might guide the aspirant in practicing a formal exercise of observation, concentration, or meditation. Or the counselor might simply encourage the aspirant to think for oneself, to doubt and question, and to separate truth from illusion. Because both participants make this invocation, there are two lines of inquiry ("carrying its dual lines of life"). There would be only one line if the aspirant passively accepted whatever explanations that the counselor might offer, or if the counselor blindly accepted whatever rationalizations, prejudices, and projections that the aspirant might offer. During a session, the counselor helps the aspirant to invoke

---

[5] Bailey, *Esoteric Healing*, pp. 707, 708.

the second-ray quality of the soul ("and its magnetic force"), which includes the aspects of both love and wisdom. The love aspect is gained by having an inclusive point of view, which means considering the needs and concerns of the aspirant's family or group rather than just those of the aspirant. The wisdom aspect is gained by going beyond the outer symptoms of the aspirant's distress, such as depression, hostility, or anxiety, and inquiring into the underlying cause or meaning.

The second sentence describes the topics or content of the counseling sessions and the order in which these topics are generally addressed. The first topic is the aspirant's physical health. The counselor and aspirant invoke understanding about how to withdraw energy from negative habits and how to establish or reinforce positive habits of behavior on the seventh or physical plane ("Let that magnetic living force withdraw and supplement that which is present in the seventh"). For instance, it is important to eliminate any dependencies on tobacco, alcohol, and other types of addictive substances. It is also important to establish or reinforce the habits of personal hygiene, balanced and nutritious diet, adequate sleep, regular physical exercise, and moderate exposure to sunshine.

Feelings of guilt, fear, or resentment imply a separation or division between the higher emotional nature—which is associated with the fourth or buddhic plane—and the emotional body—which is on the sixth or emotional plane. The second topic is how to remove or oppose this inner separation ("opposing four and six"). For instance, by observing oneself in an objective way, one can become sensitive to the various parts of one's personality and appreciate their interrelatedness. By refusing to judge or resent others, one can release oneself from one's own self-judgments and self-condemnations. By giving up attachment or desire for material possessions, one can become free from many forms of fear and suffering. By practicing harmlessness in thoughts and speech, one can become a channel for the love aspect of the soul. And by living as the soul, one can experience peace, compassion, joy, and inner confidence. The key to progress in any of these areas is self-discipline combined with a conscious understanding of the work to be done.

When one dominates or intentionally harms other people, a separation exists between one's inherent altruistic nature—which is associated with the third or atmic plane—and outer behavior—which is on the seventh or physical plane. The third topic is how to remove or oppose this second type of separation ("to three and seven"). For instance, one might learn the principles of ethics that have been taught by great philosophers from both the East and the West.

As an Eastern example, consider the system of raja yoga that was originally formulated by the sage Patanjali. The Sanskrit word *raja* means "kingly" and the word *yoga* means "union." Raja yoga is a traditional Eastern method of integrating the personality (or lower self) with the soul (or higher self), and it requires controlling and disciplining the mind. In his *Yoga Sutras,* Patanjali indicated that moral discipline was a fundamental prerequisite and that it must be achieved before mental discipline can become possible. The needed moral discipline consists of voluntary obedience to five precepts: act harmlessly, speak truthfully, do not steal, abstain from incontinence or sexual impurity, and do not covet. Similar precepts can be found in Buddhism and Christianity.[6]

As a Western example, consider the ethical philosophy of Immanuel Kant. In his effort to seek out and establish "the supreme principle of morality," Kant described several versions of what he called a "categorical imperative." Here, the word *imperative* means a directive to act in a certain way and *categorical* means unqualified or unconditional. According to the best known version of the imperative, "Act as if the maxim of your action were to become through your will a universal law of nature." In other words, one ought to avoid behavior that, if adopted by all

---

[6] C. Johnston, *The Yoga Sutras of Patanjali* (London: Stuart & Watkins, 1968), p. 43.

human beings, would make social life impossible. For instance, one should not lie or steal because social life would be impossible if everyone lied or stole.[7]

After learning the principles associated with each of the foregoing topics, the aspirant can apply those principles by using the mind to direct the activities of the emotional and physical bodies. The aspirant's next step is learning how the soul can take the dominating position and direct the mind. This step requires listening for the intuitive voice of the soul and then following that voice. To take this more advanced step, the aspirant must give up all external guides—such as any teacher or organized teaching—and replace them with the inner guidance of the soul. Counseling can not deal with this more advanced step, which involves integrating the abstract and concrete levels of the fifth or mental plane ("but dealing not with five"), because the counselor acts as an external guide during a counseling session. The point is that the aspirant must eventually become his or her own guide and find the way *alone.* Out of this aloneness, which is the lot of every true disciple, are born the self-knowledge and self-reliance needed for spiritual development.[8]

The last sentence in the first paragraph indicates the process or method of addressing a topic. There are seven steps, and each step expresses the quality of the corresponding ray. In the first step, the counselor imposes a mental boundary around some chosen topic, which is a particular physical, emotional, or ethical problem that the aspirant is confronting. In other words, the counselor helps the aspirant to keep the inquiry focussed within a predetermined confining circle that excludes all extraneous and irrelevant thoughts ("The circular"). In the second step, the counselor helps the aspirant to

[7] I. Kant, *Ethical Philosophy* (1785; reprint; Indianapolis, IN: Hackett Publishing Company, 1988), pp. 5, 30.
[8] A. A. Bailey, A *Treatise on White Magic* (1934; reprint; New York: Lucis Publishing Company, 1974), pp. 583, 584.

shift from a self-centered point of view to an inclusive one, which is the vantage point of the soul ("inclusive"). These two steps essentially guide and assist the aspirant in practicing raja yoga. The first step corresponds to the concentration stage of raja yoga, and it aligns the physical brain and the mind. The second step corresponds to the meditation stage, and it aligns the mind and the soul. When both the counselor and aspirant accomplish these stages together, there is a temporary blending and focussing of the lights of their brains, minds, and souls, thereby creating one unified light—a searchlight of great brilliance and strength ("vortex").

The third step is maintaining the mental searchlight for a sufficiently long time so that it descends to the underlying cause or meaning of the aspirant's problem ("descending to the point"). Because this cause is generally something that the aspirant wishes to repress or not acknowledge as being true, the fourth step is a period in which the aspirant reacts in a disturbed, defensive, and resentful manner ("disturbs"). The aspirant should be helped to realize that such reactions are not a sign of failure but are expected in the healing process. In fact, the fifth step in the process is making the aspirant's disturbance the temporary topic of investigation. The counselor and aspirant need to examine those reactions until their joint inquiry clarifies and removes them ("removes").

The sixth step is returning to the original problem of investigation. Because the aspirant can now examine the underlying cause without being disturbed or defensive, the joint inquiry next supplies a solution to the problem ("and then supplies"). This solution is generally a deep understanding and appreciation of some physical, emotional, or ethical principle of living. In the seventh and final step, the counselor assists the aspirant in demonstrating the truth of that principle in daily life ("and thus the work is done").

The final paragraph in the formula describes the participants of a counseling session, both visible and invisible. The first participant is the aspirant. The type of inner conflict being faced by the aspirant determines the counseling approach that is appropriate. The approach described in the present section is suitable only when the aspirant is on the path of probation and therefore is facing an inner conflict between personality and soul. Before the path of probation, the activity of the heart chakra is almost negligible. As progress is made on this path, the heart chakra gradually becomes active. Bailey's formula symbolizes the aspirant with a heart chakra that has started to become active ("The heart revolves").[9]

The counselor is the second participant. Ideally, he or she has already worked through the same types of problems that the aspirant is now confronting, mastered the stages of raja yoga, and attained the first initiation, which is equivalent to completing the path of probation. In any case, the counselor and aspirant ought to have sufficient openness and rapport so that their inquiries are a synergistic collaboration ("two hearts revolve as one"). They need to take the journey together, seeking to understand the inner causes that lie behind the aspirant's outer symptoms.

While traveling on the path of probation, the aspirant has an incorporeal teacher who resides on the inner planes of consciousness. This incorporeal teacher is called the "spirit guide" in spiritualism and is referred to by Bailey as "the senior disciple who has the neophyte in charge." When communicating guidance, the spirit guide instills the needed intuitive message within the aspirant's soul. If the aspirant has sufficient alignment or integration between personality and soul, the message quickly finds its way into the consciousness of the personality, perhaps at the time of communication or later during the same day. But if the aspirant is at an early stage and lacks alignment, the message from the spirit guide often requires a long period, perhaps many years, to bring through an adequate recognition within the mind and brain. In either case, the aspirant might receive intuitive instruction on how to learn about personal weaknesses and correct them. Or the aspirant might receive

---

[9] Bailey, *Esoteric Psychology*, vol. 2, pp. 524, 525.

suggestions that lead to books or specific written passages that teach and elucidate, or to people in the physical environment who can provide assistance.[10]

The concept of heart is sometimes symbolized by the number "twelve." For instance, Table 1 (on page 16) shows that the heart chakra is the only one having exactly twelve petals. This table also shows that the crown chakra is depicted with two circles of petals: an inner circle consisting of twelve petals and an outer circle consisting of 960 petals. The inner circle is called the "heart center in the head," because it is the higher correspondence of the heart chakra and is also the intermediary between the crown chakra and the soul.[11] According to Bailey, "the soul is the heart of the system of the spiritual man," because it is the source of the consciousness and life that animate the personality.[12] As discussed in more detail in the fourth-ray section of chapter 3, the soul is also symbolized by a twelve-petalled lotus called the egoic lotus. The next part of the formula uses these three twelve-petalled lotuses to represent different participants in a counseling session.

Lacking alignment with both the soul and spirit guide, the aspirant has sought the temporary assistance of the counselor on the physical plane. If the counselor has sufficient alignment, then he or she can intuitively receive the necessary instruction from the aspirant's spirit guide and then convey that instruction through his or her own words and thoughts. In this circumstance, the aspirant's spirit guide is the third participant in the counseling session, and a therapeutic triangle is formed between the aspirant, whose heart chakra is activated as a result of the instruction ("the twelve within the vehicle"); the

---

[10] A. A. Bailey, *Discipleship in the New Age,* vol. 1 (1944; reprint; New York: Lucis Publishing Company, 1976), pp. 723, 724; M. Bailey, A *Learning Experience* (New York: Lucis Publishing Company, 1990), pp. 17-26.

[11] A. A. Bailey, *The Light of the Soul* (1955; reprint; New York: Lucis Publishing Company, 1978), p. 293; Bailey, *Esoteric Healing,* pp. 157, 160, 170.

[12] A. A. Bailey, *Discipleship in the New Age,* vol. 2 (1955; reprint; New York: Lucis Publishing Company, 1972), p. 289.

counselor, who intuitively receives the instruction via the heart center in the head ("the twelve within the head"); and the spirit guide, who works on the soul level transmitting the instruction from soul to soul ("and the twelve upon the plane of soul endeavor").

Neither the counselor nor the aspirant may be aware of the existence of the spirit guide on the inner planes of consciousness. Instead, the counselor may simply be aware of having an intuitive hunch, and the aspirant may simply be impressed by the seemingly insightful nature of the counselor. In any case, when all three points of the therapeutic triangle cooperate in an integrated way, the aspirant receives the needed assistance ("cooperate as one and thus the work is done").

Four kingdoms of nature are present in the physical world. The first kingdom is the mineral, the second is the vegetable, the third is the animal, and the fourth is the human. In addition, there is the fifth or spiritual kingdom—which is called the "kingdom of God" by Christians and the "spiritual Hierarchy of our planet" by theosophists. This spiritual kingdom exists on the inner planes and is starting to externalize on the physical plane. Members of the fifth kingdom are called "Masters of the Wisdom." These Masters were once members of the human kingdom. But by learning the needed lessons in the fourth kingdom, they attained what in theosophy is called the fifth initiation and thereby passed into the fifth kingdom.

The spiritual kingdom is organized into various inner ashrams or schools, each of which is directed by a Master of the Wisdom. Because the aspirant is assumed to be on the path of probation, he or she has reached the periphery of one of the inner ashrams. As a result, the Master of that ashram has assigned a senior member of the ashram, the spirit guide, to watch over the aspirant and provide appropriate assistance. The spirit guide is not yet a Master but is more advanced than the aspirant. When a person achieves the first initiation, he or she is admitted into the ashram and thereby earns the privilege of receiving intuitive instruction and guidance directly from the Master. But while still on the path of probation, the aspirant is under the tutelage of the spirit guide, who in turn reports to and receives instruction from the Master.[13]

The fourth participant in a counseling session is the Master of the ashram that is being approached by the aspirant. Although not participating directly in a session, the Master participates indirectly by sending a steady flow of teaching toward the inner spirit guide and another flow of teaching toward the outer counselor, provided that the latter has attained the first initiation and is a member of the same ashram ("Two energies achieve this consummation"). Each flow of teaching helps the recipient to become detached from the form side of life, become impersonal when dealing with others, cooperate with those engaged in similar work, and become prepared for greater expansions of consciousness in the future. Through the influence of these two flows of teaching, the aspirant, counselor, and spirit guide ("and the three whose number is a twelve") respond to the purpose and plan of the Master ("respond to the greater twelve"). Because the Master can be considered as the heart of the inner ashram, the formula represents this last participant as the "greater twelve."[14]

In conclusion, the second-ray formula presents several precepts for counseling someone on the path of probation. When these precepts are applied, the aspirant discovers the underlying meaning of the problems in his or her life ("The life is known") and spends more time displaying the wisdom of the soul ("and the years prolonged").

Ray Three

The healer stands and weaves. He gathers from the three, the five, the seven that which is needed for the

---

[13] Bailey, *Discipleship in the New Age,* vol. 1, pp. 723, 724.
[14] Bailey, *Discipleship in the New Age,* vol. 1, pp. 737, 738.

heart of life. He brings the energies together and makes
them serve the third; he thus creates a vortex into which
the one distressed must descend and with him goes
the healer. And yet they both remain in peace and
calm. Thus must the angel of the Lord descend into
the pool and bring the healing life.[15]

The name of the third ray is active intelligence or adaptability. In the method described by the third-ray formula, the
healer evokes the third-ray quality of the soul and then prepares an educational environment that evokes the same quality within the patients. We shall refer to the healer as the
teacher and the patient as the child, because we shall interpret
this formula as describing the well-known Montessori method
of early childhood education.

Maria Montessori was born in Italy in 1870 and became
the first woman in that country to receive a medical degree,
graduating from the University of Rome Medical School in 1896.
Because she was convinced that mentally retarded children could
profit from special education, she became the director of the
state school for children committed to insane asylums. During
the two years that she spent teaching there, Montessori began
developing her educational system. She made careful observations of the children, prepared new educational materials,
took notes, and reflected on her progress. To her amazement,
she found that these severely retarded children could be
taught many things that were previously thought impossible.
Later, Montessori became the director of a day-care center in
a housing project located in a slum. The children who attended
this center had normal intelligence but came from econom-
ically and socially deprived backgrounds and from illiterate parents. She continued with her educational experiments at this
center and achieved remarkable results.

---

[15] Bailey, *Esoteric Healing,* p. 708.

Information about Montessori's achievements spread quickly. She opened additional schools, some of which enrolled children from wealthy and literate parents. Visitors started to come and they were impressed by the discipline, concentrated attention, spontaneity, and progress of the children. She started publicizing her revolutionary ideas through lectures, teacher-training courses, and numerous books. Her philosophy and schools eventually spread to all continents of the world, especially throughout Europe and India. After receiving many honorary degrees and tributes, Montessori died in the Netherlands in 1952, shortly before her eighty-second birthday.

The following is a description of Montessori's educational principles, using an interpretation of the symbolic formula for the third ray. The quotations that are not within parentheses are taken from Montessori's own writings. The quotations that are within parentheses refer to Bailey's formula.

First, the Montessori teacher begins by preparing herself inwardly. This preparation includes examining herself, diminishing egocentric and authoritarian attitudes, cultivating "a kind of faith that the child will reveal himself through work," and "rising to spiritual heights"[16] ("The healer stands"). The teacher also cultivates the mental attitudes of "rigorous observation" and experimentation, which have the effect of evoking the active intelligence of her soul ("and weaves"). "Such a preparation should generate in her consciousness a conception of life capable of transforming her, of calling forth in her a special 'activity,' an 'aptitude' which shall make her efficient for her task."[17]

After preparing herself inwardly, the teacher is ready to prepare the classroom environment so that it meets the needs

---

[16] M. Montessori, *The Absorbent Mind* (1949; reprint; New York: Dell, 1984), pp. 270, 274.

[17] M. Montessori *The Advanced Montessori Method,* vol. 1 (1916; reprint; New York: Schocken Books, 1965), pp. 138, 139.

of the children. The enumeration in the second sentence refers to the seven planes and symbolizes the various types of learning that should be promoted in the classroom. The third—or atmic plane—is the home of spiritual volition and ethical behavior; the fifth—or mental plane—is the home of intellectual abilities and knowledge; and the seventh—or physical plane—is the home of physical coordination, exercise, and activity. When preparing the classroom environment, the teacher includes the volitional, intellectual, and physical elements needed for developing the inner potential of the children ("He gathers from the three, the five, the seven that which is needed for the heart of life"). We shall discuss each of these elements in the given order.

According to Montessori, volition or will is a universal force that could be defined as an urge to purposeful activity.

> In the little child's life, as soon as he makes an action deliberately, of his own accord, this force has begun to enter into his consciousness. What we call his will has begun to develop, and this process continues henceforward, but only as a result of experience. Hence, we are beginning to think of the will not as something inborn, but as something which has to be developed and, because it is a part of nature, this development can only occur in obedience to natural laws.[18]

Montessori felt that the development of willpower is a slow process that evolves through activity in relationship to the environment. The volitional elements of the classroom (those that are gathered "from the three") are appropriate activities through which children can develop their willpower. To achieve physical independence, children have opportunities to take care of their own personal needs, such as washing themselves or cleaning their clothes. They should not be served by others in acts that they can learn to perform for themselves. To develop their

---

[18] Montessori, *The Absorbent Mind,* p. 248.

independent wills, children have opportunities for choice and constructive work. They need to learn how to make decisions, bringing into motion complex internal processes of comparison and judgment, and to learn how to coordinate their activities toward self-chosen ends. To develop the capacity of independent thought, they are allowed to work without interruption and to repeat any exercise until they are satisfied with their own mastery. To develop a social concern and helpfulness for others, children have as much freedom as possible in their social relations, being able to speak to each other and initiate activities together whenever they wish. However, the teacher should stop or "check in the child whatever offends or annoys others, or whatever tends toward rough or ill-bred acts."[19]

The intellectual elements of the Montessori classroom consist of educational materials and fall into two categories: academic and artistic. The academic materials are for teaching reading, writing, mathematics, geography, and science; their purpose is to satisfy the children's innate desire to develop intellectual abilities and learn about the world. The artistic materials deal with self-expression and the communication of ideas—such as through music, drawing, and sculpture. After a brief introduction on how to use each artistic medium, the children are left to freely develop their own creativity.

The physical elements of the Montessori classroom are also educational materials and fall into two categories: practical living and sensorial. The children are initially introduced to the materials of practical living, which provide exercises concerning the physical care of oneself and one's environment. For instance, they might learn how to shine their shoes or wash a table. Next, they are introduced to some of the sensorial materials, which provide visual, tactile, auditory, olfactory, gustatory, thermic, baric, stereognostic, and chromatic experiences.

---

[19] Montessori *The Absorbent Mind,* p. 275; M. Montessori, *The Montessori Method* (1909; reprint; New York: Schocken Books, 1964), p. 87.

The Montessori educational materials, whether of an intellectual or physical nature, ideally share six characteristics. First, these materials are meaningful to the children in the sense of being able to capture their attention and evoke a process of concentration. Second, each lesson that the child is to discover and understand is isolated in a single piece of material without being mixed with other issues. For instance, a tower of blocks presents to the child only a variation in size from block to block, rather than a combined variation in size, shape, and color. Third, the design or usage of the materials becomes progressively more complex. For instance, a series of ten rods with varying lengths are initially used as a sensorial exercise to teach the meaning of length. Later the same rods are used to teach addition, subtraction, multiplication, and division. Fourth, the materials are designed to prepare children indirectly for future learning. A good example is the development of writing. By lifting and manipulating knobs, children learn to coordinate the motor action of their fingers and thumbs. By making designs that are guided by metal patterns, they develop the ability to use a pencil. Thus, when eventually they are motivated to write, they can do so with little frustration. Fifth, the materials begin as concrete expressions of ideas and then gradually become more abstract. For instance, the idea of a triangle might begin as a solid wooden triangle that can be sensorially explored. Later, a child moves to flat wooden triangles that can be fitted into wooden puzzle boxes, then to paper triangles filled with solid colors, and then to thinly outlined triangles on paper. And sixth, since the Montessori materials are designed for self-education, they are prepared so that children can recognize their own errors when working with them, rather than having those errors pointed out by someone else.[20]

---

[20] P. P. Lillard, *Montessori: A Modern Approach* (New York: Schocken Books, 1972), pp. 60-63.

The Montessori teacher brings the volitional, intellectual, and physical elements together in a classroom environment that is suitable for the children ("He brings the energies together"). Through careful observation and experimentation, the teacher ensures that the classroom evokes the active intelligence or third-ray quality of each child's soul, which is the inner capacity for constructive self-development ("and makes them serve the third"). "All the physical or intrinsic qualities of the objects should be determined, not only by the immediate reaction of attention they provoke in the child, but also by their . . . power of evoking the effective collaboration of the highest activities (comparison, judgement)."[21] Thus, the teacher's influence on the children is primarily indirect. Rather than directly imparting information and facts, the teacher prepares a special environment into which the children enter, enabling them to learn and grow through their own self-efforts ("he thus creates a vortex into which the one distressed must descend"). As pointed out by Montessori, "however much you speak and speak and speak, you accomplish nothing because the child cannot take directly but only indirectly."[22]

Nevertheless, the teacher remains present with the children to observe them and to introduce the materials ("and with him goes the healer"). Any item should be presented at the right moment in a child's development and its introduction is called "the fundamental lesson." This lesson not only presents a child with a key to the new material and possibilities, but it enables the teacher to discover more about the child. In this sense, "the lesson corresponds to an experiment."[23] Such lessons are generally given on an individual basis, because no two children are likely to be exactly at the same point of devel-

---

[21] Montessori, *The Advanced Montessori Method*, vol. 1, p. 75.

[22] M. Montessori, *Reconstruction in Education* (1948; reprint; Wheaton, IL: Theosophical Press, 1964), p. 10.

[23] Montessori, *The Montessori Method*, p. 107.

opment. Choosing the right moment to introduce a lesson requires sensitivity and experience, since the teacher is momentarily taking the initiative away from the child.

> In such a delicate task, a great art must suggest the moment, and limit the intervention, in order that we shall arouse no perturbation, cause no deviation, but rather that we shall help the soul which is coming into the fullness of life, and which shall live from its *own forces*.[24]

Except for stopping offensive behavior and introducing new materials, the teacher is only an observer and avoids all interference with the child ("And yet they both remain in peace and calm"). According to Montessori, "Praise, help, or even a look, may be enough to interrupt him, or destroy the activity. It seems a strange thing to say, but this can happen even if the child merely becomes aware of being watched."[25] With this freedom, the children are able to choose their own activities and set their own pace for working with the educational materials.

After the third-ray quality is evoked from within each child, it descends into the classroom in the form of purposeful, intelligent, and coordinated work ("Thus must the angel of the Lord descend into the pool"). This work brings self-improvement, integration, and fulfillment of the inner pattern with which the children were born ("and bring the healing life"). Because their work has satisfied an inner need, the children appear pleased, peaceful, and rested after their strenuous labors. Montessori emphasizes "that the joy of the child is in accomplishing things great for his age; that the real satisfaction of the child is to give maximum effort to the task in hand; that happiness consists

---

[24] Montessori, *The Montessori Method,* p. 115.
[25] Montessori, *The Absorbent Mind,* pp. 273, 274.

in well directed activity of body and mind in the way of excellence; that strength of mind and body and spirit is acquired by exercise and experience."[26]

The Montessori approach to education has been widely used with much success for many types of children, but it is especially appropriate as a method of personality integration for children with handicaps and deprivations. As noted earlier, Montessori began her work first with mentally retarded children and then with children from very impoverished backgrounds. Because such children may have had very little prior learning, she built into her method the simplest of life's activities: how to wash, dress, carry things, hear, touch, and see. Children from deprived backgrounds are often surrounded by despair and defeat, and they have difficulty in developing trust in life or in their own powers. Montessori's emphasis on constructive work helps such children to develop a positive self-image. When they achieve success on their own with the materials in the classroom, they learn to appreciate their own worth and abilities. Her stress on the inner preparation of teachers is also important. By cultivating a spirit of faith in children from any background, a teacher will have the attitude needed for awakening their love and interest.[27]

Ray Four

The healer knows the place where dissonance is found. He also knows the power of sound and the sound which must be heard. Knowing the note to which the fourth great group reacts and linking it to the great Creative Nine, he sounds the note which brings

---

[26] M. Montessori, *What You Should Know About Your Child* (1948; reprint; Madras, India: Kalakshetra Publications, 1961), p. 131.

[27] Lillard, *Montessori: A Modern Approach,* pp. 143, 144.

release, the note which will bring absorption into one. He educates the listening ear of him who must be healed; he likewise trains the listening ear of him who must go forth. He knows the manner of the sound which brings the healing touch; and also that which says: Depart. And thus the work is done.[28]

The name of the fourth ray is harmony through conflict, and its basic quality is unification. In the literal interpretation of the fourth-ray formula, various types of sounds are employed to bring harmony in several conflicted situations. Because Bailey states that "sound is colour and colour is sound,"[29] we shall interpret the fourth formula as describing the process of healing through either sounds or colors. From the viewpoint of physics, sound and color are closely related because both are manifestations of a single fundamental phenomenon called vibration. Sound and light waves differ, however, with respect to their rate of vibration and medium of transmission.

The first two sentences in the formula describe three preliminary steps for using sounds or colors in healing. First, the healer diagnoses the discordant condition, identifying the specific needs and area of distress ("The healer knows the place where dissonance is found"). Second, the healer determines the specific sounds or colors that have the power to alleviate the distress ("He also knows the power of sound"). And third, the healer determines how to apply those sounds or colors in such a way that they must be heard or seen by the recipients, enabling the healing to occur ("and the sound which must be heard").

The next three sentences describe five different areas of application for sounds or colors in healing. To understand the first sentence, it is necessary to review some background infor-

---

[28] Bailey, *Esoteric Healing,* p. 709.
[29] A. A. Bailey, *Letters on Occult Meditation* (1922; reprint; New York: Lucis Publishing Company, 1974), p. 205.

mation regarding service activities of human beings. According to Bailey, there are nine different types of service groups plus a synthesizing tenth type that consists of representatives from the other nine. Table 2 (on page 38) lists and describes the nine types of service groups. Each type has an inner counterpart within the fifth or spiritual kingdom of nature. Outer human groups of the same type are disjointed fragments, but the associated spiritual group is a completed whole. Each outer group attempts to manifest a specific type of energy that is embodied by its inner counterpart. Depending on the outer group, the manifesting energy may be in the form of vital healing forces, scientific discoveries, or new ideas in education, politics, religion, or economics. For such a manifestation to occur, the outer human group must first achieve unity within itself and then achieve unity with its inner spiritual counterpart.[30]

In the first area of application, sounds or colors are used as part of a ritual to unify a group of human beings who wish to provide service to the world. No group work is ever possible without the members participating in some form of ritual that produces uniformity of action. Through experimentation, the healer gains knowledge about the specific sounds or colors to which members of the fourth or human kingdom of nature respond ("Knowing the note to which the fourth great group reacts") and that links the members with the nine specialized service groups within the spiritual kingdom ("and linking it to the great Creative Nine"). Afterwards, the healer conducts one ritual to help the members of an outer group release their individual concerns and achieve unity among themselves ("he sounds the note which brings release"). The members must learn to cooperate with each other, subordinating their own ideas of personal growth to the group requirements. Next, the healer conducts another ritual to help the members

---

[30] A. A. Bailey, *The Externalisation of the Hierarchy*, (1957; reprint; New York: Lucis Publishing Company, 1976), pp. 38, 47; Bailey, *Esoteric Psychology*, vol. 2, pp. 182, 193, 194.

Table 2. Nine Types of Service Groups.*

Number	Name	Description
1	Telepathic Communicators	"These people are receptive to impression from the Masters and from each other; they are the custodians of group purpose and, therefore, closely related to all the other types of groups."
2	Trained Observers	"Their objective is to see clearly through all events, through space and time by means of the cultivation and use of the intuition."
3	Magnetic Healers	"They work intelligently with the vital force of the etheric body . . . . The work to be done is that of the intelligent transmission of energy to various parts of the nature—mental, emotional and physical."
4	Educators of the New Age	"Their service is along the line of culture and they will work to bring in the new type of education. Their emphasis will be upon the building of the antahkarana and upon the use of the mind in meditation."
5	Political Observers	"They will work in the world of human government, dealing with the problems of civilisation and with the relationship existing between nations. The bringing about of international understanding will be their major objective."

Table 2. Nine Types of Service Groups (continued).*

Number	Name	Description
6	Workers in the Field of Religion	"Their work is to formulate the universal platform of the new world religion. It is a work of loving synthesis and it will emphasize the unity and the fellowship of the spirit."
7	Scientific Servers	"They will reveal the essential spirituality of all scientific work which is motivated by love of humanity and its welfare, which relates science and religion and brings to light the glory of God through the medium of His tangible world and His works."
8	Psychologists	"Their major task will be to relate, through approved techniques, the soul and the personality, leading to the revelation of divinity through the medium of humanity. They will act also as transmitters of illumination between groups of thinkers and as illuminators of group thought."
9	Financiers and Economists	"They will work with the energies and forces which express themselves through the interchange and the values of commerce; they will deal with Law of Supply and Demand and with the great principle of *Sharing* which ever governs divine purpose."

*Source: A. A. Bailey, *Discipleship in the New Age,* vol. 1 (1944; reprint; New York: Lucis Publishing Company, 1976), pp. 35-40.

become absorbed in the single purpose of serving humanity ("the note which will bring absorption into one"). When the group succeeds in fusing itself with this purpose, it becomes united with its inner counterpart within the spiritual kingdom and thus is able to receive inspiration and guidance from that more evolved group.[31]

Many approaches are possible for using sounds in a group ritual. For instance, the sense of group unity can be promoted by singing or listening to any music that expresses collective emotions or aspirations, such as national anthems, religious hymns, marches, and folk songs. According to Roberto Assagioli, the highest and most effective expression of this type of music is Beethoven's Ninth Symphony, which includes a chorus calling for universal brotherhood.[32] Thirty-five years after Assagioli first published that assessment, journalists reported that Beethoven's Ninth Symphony was the primary unifying music used by the Chinese democracy movement in 1989 and the Lithuanian independence movement in 1990. Other examples of the use of sounds in a group ritual include saying or chanting in unison pledges of allegiance, prayers, affirmations, or Sanskrit mantras.

Many approaches are also possible for using colors in a group ritual. Priests and ministers often have colorful robes and conduct ceremonies that involve lighting candles. A military army or marching band achieves a sense of group unity by wearing uniforms consisting of the same color. A leader of a meditation group might guide the members in visualizing a particular sequence of symbols and colors.

The next sentence in the formula describes the second area of application. By using appropriate sounds or colors, the healer trains or conditions the emotional body of a patient who

---

[31] A. A. Bailey, *Esoteric Psychology*, vol. 1 (1936; reprint; New York: Lucis Publishing Company, 1975), p. 363; A. A. Bailey, *The Rays and the Initiations* (1960; reprint; New York: Lucis Publishing Company, 1976), pp. 211-213.
[32] R. Assagioli, M.D., *Psychosynthesis* (1965; reprint; New York: Penguin Books, 1987), p. 250.

must be healed by some other means ("He educates the listening ear of him who must be healed"). For instance, suppose that the patient needs to receive surgery or dental treatment. Music is often used to help such patients relax and feel at ease, and some major hospitals have used music to hasten or facilitate anesthesia in their operating rooms. Music is especially helpful for patients who are so tense and nervous that the routine medical sedatives are not very effective and for patients who are too old or ill to receive sedatives. In any case, the music should be soft, slow, and soothing. It is also important to have the right colors for the walls and furnishings. For instance, certain shades of blue have a soothing, calming, harmonizing effect.[33]

As a second example, suppose that the patient needs to receive psychotherapy. The use of appropriate music can help promote two major objectives of psychotherapy: bringing into awareness psychological elements that have been repressed; and releasing and transmuting certain instinctual and emotional energies. Depending on its specific purpose, music can be used before, during, or after the psychotherapeutic treatment. The use of appropriate colors can also help promote the same objectives, because a color can have a stimulating, recuperative, or sedative effect.[34]

The next sentence in the formula refers to death. Hindus and Buddhists generally believe that the last thought at the moment of death determines the future of the soul. For instance, Sri Krishna in the *Bhagavad Gita* says, "For whatever object a man thinks of at the final moment, when he leaves his body—that alone does he obtain."[35] According to this belief, life always continues after physical death, but how we die determines whether we have immediate illumination, our need to reincarnate, and the conditions for our next incarnation. If this belief is true, then a dying person should make a strenuous effort to

---

[33] Assagioli, *Psychosynthesis,* pp. 247, 256, 285.

[34] Assagioli, *Psychosynthesis,* pp. 256, 257, 286.

[35] Swami Nikhilananda, *The Bhagavad Gita* (1944; reprint; New York: Ramakrishna-Vivekananda Center, 1969), p. 199.

face death calmly and clearly, have an intellect rightly trained and directed, and transcend mentally any bodily pain. Eastern traditions emphasize the value of influencing dying persons in a positive way, helping them to achieve success in their last experiences of physical life.

In the third area of application, the healer trains the consciousness of someone who is dying and must go forth into the after-death experience ("he likewise trains the listening ear of him who must go forth"). Several approaches are possible here. The healer might play certain types of music, primarily music with one constantly recurring chord, or might audibly chant certain mantra phrases with the purpose of building those phrases into the consciousness of the dying person. In Tibetan Buddhism, a monk would recite passages from the *Tibetan Book of the Dead,* which is a book of instructions for the dead and the dying.[36]

The use of colors can also be helpful. For instance, if the dying person has no possibility of recovery, then it would be desirable to install orange lights in the sick room. Because orange facilitates attentiveness and alertness, installing this color helps the dying person to withdraw out of the physical body in full waking awareness. If the person is able to withdraw consciously, no hiatus occurs between the sense of awareness on the physical plane and that of the after-death state. One remains aware of all phenomena connected with the dying process. After the transition occurs, one knows oneself to be the same as before, though without an apparatus whereby one can contact the physical world. Meanwhile the physical body is left silent and empty, and it starts to disintegrate.[37]

To understand the next sentence in Bailey's formula, it is necessary to review some information regarding vibration. Every physical body (such as wood, metal, or living flesh) vibrates according to some particular measure, keynote, or nat-

---

[36] W. Y. Evans-Wentz, *The Tibetan Book of the Dead* (third edition; New York: Oxford University Press, 1957).

[37] Bailey, *A Treatise on White Magic,* pp. 498, 505-507.

ural frequency, although this vibration may be imperceptible to normal human faculties. The natural frequency of a body is determined by its shape, mass, weight, and molecular construction. When a sound wave of one frequency strikes a body that will vibrate at the same frequency, the vibration of the body is called *sympathetic vibration*. The reinforcement of sound resulting from sympathetic vibration is called *resonance*. When a sound wave causes a body to vibrate sympathetically at a frequency that is not its own natural frequency, the vibration of the body is known as *forced vibration*.

For instance, if you were to tap the edge of wine glass, the resulting tone would show the natural frequency of that glass. If a singer matched her pitch to the exact frequency of the glass, the sympathetic vibration imposed on the glass could cause it to shatter. As another example, suppose that you tuned two violins, held one, and placed the other several feet away. If you were to draw a bow over a string in the violin that you held, then that string would vibrate at its own natural frequency. Furthermore, the corresponding string belonging to the other violin would also begin to sound, illustrating both sympathetic vibration and resonance.

In the fourth area of application, the healer uses appropriate sounds or colors that bring physical or emotional healing to the patient ("He knows the manner of sound which brings the healing touch"). Let us consider some methods that bring about physical healing. First of all, sounds with a specific tone or frequency can directly affect the physical body of the patient. As discussed in the preceding paragraphs, each organ or body structure has its own natural frequency. Illness may occur in an organ when it is forced to vibrate at a frequency different from its true natural frequency. The healing approach is to determine the natural frequency of a diseased organ and then apply sounds with that frequency. The sympathetic vibration imposed on the diseased organ then causes the organ to return to its natural frequency, which may restore health.[38]

---

[38] R. McClellan, Ph.D., *The Healing Forces of Music* (Amity, NY: Amity House, 1988), pp. 48, 49.

When using specific frequencies for healing, we can generate the sounds in two different ways: through a source outside the patient, such as a musical instrument, voice, or specialized electronic device; or through the patient's own voice. In any case, we should have accurate knowledge regarding the exact tone to transmit. For instance, the natural frequency, in terms of cycles per second, is known for several organs in the body including the brain and heart. According to tantra yoga, the chanting of the right mantra sound can energize and balance any given chakra. Randall McClellan associates each of the endocrine glands with a specific vowel sound and pitch. By using a special instrument for generating the desired frequencies, Peter Guy Manners, an osteopath, has treated rheumatic conditions, arthritis, fractures, muscle strain, whiplash, slipped discs, fibrositis, and paralysis. Much more experimental research must be performed, however, before this method of healing can be applied with any confidence.[39]

Sounds in the form of suggestive treatment can also bring about physical healing. The underlying theory here is that three types of mind affect the health of the physical body: the conscious, subconscious, and cellular minds. The *conscious mind* is concerned with what one believes or knows to be true about oneself—qualities, characteristics, powers, tendencies, and achievements. The *subconscious mind* governs one's instinctual nature and has several layers: all suppressed and unrecognized desires, guilts, and urges; all inherited tendencies and innate predispositions; the management and coordination of all bodily processes including digestion, assimilation, and elimination; and the group consciousness of the sum-total of bodily cells. The *cellular mind* is the intelligence of an individual cell in the body, and it displays instinctive knowledge, adaptation, and memory. Suggestive treatment can change the beliefs of the conscious mind and instruct the subconscious

---

[39] McClellan, *The Healing Forces of Music,* pp. 41, 49, 53, 54, 67-71, 90-92.

mind. Afterward, the subconscious mind can reorganize the activities of the many organs and cells, which brings about the physical healing.[40]

Yogi Ramacharaka gives the healer the following rules for suggestive treatment. Cultivate in yourself an attitude of earnestness—which means have the best interests of the patient at heart. Act with this purpose, be concentrated, and have self-confidence. Also cultivate a firm powerful gaze in your eyes and a good suggestive voice—which means that strength, feeling, and earnestness are in the tone. Place the patient in an easy, comfortable position, and help him or her maintain a calm, relaxed, and peaceful frame of mind. Give the treatment in surroundings that are not distracting, so that the patient can give his or her entire attention to the treatment. Repeat the key ideas of the treatment again and again, not in a monotonous way but in varying arrangements of words. During the treatment, reinforce the idea of the mind's power, describe the proper and normal conditions of digestion, assimilation, and elimination, and describe the proper functioning of the specific organs causing trouble. Never make any reference to the diseased condition but always speak of the condition as you want it to be. Help the patient to picture in his or her own mind the desired and expected condition of health.[41]

Music can bring about emotional healing, because it has the power to create moods and to elicit emotional responses. Several scientific studies have investigated the mood effects of music, and several therapists have developed healing systems based on music. For instance, carefully chosen music can help a depressed person become more joyous, a nervous or agitated person become more tranquil, a solemn or serious person become more whimsical, or a shy person become more dramatic or assertive.[42]

---

[40] Bailey, *Esoteric Psychology,* vol. 2, pp. 65, 440.
[41] Yogi Ramacharaka, *The Science of Psychic Healing* (1909; reprint; Chicago: Yogi Publication Society, 1937), pp. 123-134.
[42] McClellan, *The Healing Forces of Music,* pp. 139, 140.

Table 3. The Use of Colors for Healing.*

Color	Description	Illnesses
Red	"Heating, vitalizing and stimulating vibration."	Blood-deficiency diseases, Anaemia, Physical debility, Exhaustion, Bad circulation, Paralysis, and Consumption
Orange	"Warm, positive and stimulating colour, influencing primarily the vital processes of assimilation and circulation."	Nervous and mental debility, Asthma, Bronchitis, Phlegm, and Epilepsy
Yellow	"A positive magnetic vibration with a tonic effect on the nerves."	Dyspepsia, Diabetes, and Constitipation
Green	"A vibration of harmony and balance . . . Soothing and sympathetic, it does not excite, inflame or irritate."	Heart complaints, Blood pressure, and Headaches
Blue	"Cold vibration with astringent and sleep inducing properties."	Laryngitis, Sore throat, Hoarseness, Goitre, Fevers, Palpitation, Bilious attacks, Colic, Jaundice, Skin abrasions, Cuts, and Burns
Indigo	"Expels the negative elements in the consciousness."	Deafness, Cataract, Delirium tremens, Eye inflammation, Penumonia, and Mental disorders
Violet	"Corresponds with the highest elements in man's nature."	Nervous ailments, Insomnia, Mental disorders, and Cataract

*Source: S. G. J. Ouseley, *The Powers Of The Rays: The Science Of Colour Healing* (1951; reprint; Essex, England: L. N. Fowler, 1986), pp. 69-80.

When applying music therapy, one can not prescribe a musical selection that is always appropriate for everyone having the same emotional disorder. People hearing the same music may be affected differently, because their emotional responses depend on such variables as the kind of day that they are having, their worries and cares, whether they are physically comfortable, their past associations, their familiarity with the musical idiom that the composition represents, and their personal preferences. Furthermore, their musical preferences change with the growth of their character and the unfoldment of their inner life.[43]

Colors can also bring both physical and emotional health, and they can be administered in several ways. The healer could apply colored lights directly to the patient's physical body or could use the power of thought, visualizing the patient as being bathed in a particular color. Alternatively, the patient could wear selected colors or could practice *color breathing*, which is deep rhythmic breathing combined with the visualization of a selected color.

Particular colors can affect certain diseases, alleviate specific nervous disorders and emotional tendencies, and help build new tissues. According to Bailey, orange stimulates the activity of the etheric body and removes congestion. Rose acts on the nervous system, helps to remove depression and debilitation, and increases the will to live. Green has a general healing effect, and it is helpful in cases of inflammation and fever.[44] S. G. J. Ouseley provides a more extensive discussion of color healing that is summarized in Table 3.

Sound can disrupt just as it can bring cohesion; color can destroy just as it can heal. In the fifth and final area of application, the healer uses certain sounds or colors that cause the departure of diseased tissue, constituting an alternative approach to surgery ("and also that which says: Depart"). In recent years, the medical profession has experimented with ultra-

[43] M. P. Hall, *The Therapeutic Value of Music Including the Philosophy of Music* (Los Angeles: The Philosophical Research Society, 1982), p. 13.
[44] Bailey, *Letters on Occult Meditation,* pp. 247, 248.

sonic waves, which are sound waves with frequencies above the higher limit of human hearing, and has applied those waves to perform surgery on the physical body. The list of surgical applications for this approach is varied and includes the removal of tumors, removal of kidney stones, ophthalmic surgery, partial splenectomy, and brain surgery.

The word *laser* is an acronym for light amplification by stimulated emission of radiation, and it refers to a device that generates and amplifies coherent light. In contrast to ordinary light, coherent light has a single frequency, single intensity, and a uniform wave pattern. In recent years, the medical profession has used lasers to perform many types of surgery: oral, thoracic, gynecologic, and neurosurgery; spinal and brain tumor removal; and excisional procedures in dermatology. Laser surgery is sometimes called "bloodless surgery," because it has the advantage of producing cauterization around the excision.

Mental imagery has been used by many traditional cultures for centuries to treat a wide range of physical disorders, and this approach is now being investigated in several leading scientific journals. Documented cases have shown that color, as part of a healing visualization, can remove corrupt tissue from the physical body. For instance, Gerald Epstein, a psychiatrist, reported a case in which he helped a woman treat several uterine fibroid tumors by using mental imagery. Instead of submitting to the surgery recommended by her gynecologist, she visualized the mental application of blue and gold laser lights to her tumors. After three cycles of application, she required neither surgery nor any further trips to the gynecologist for her condition. The complete visualization that she used is as follows:

> Close your eyes. Breathe out three times. See yourself entering your body by any opening you choose. Take a light with you. Find your way to your uterus and examine the fibroids to determine their location, size, and color. Bring a tube of blue laser light and focus it directly at the fibroids, seeing them shrink

and shrivel up, then direct a tube of golden laser light around the base of the fibroids and laser-surgically excise the fibroids that remained after using the blue laser light. See the golden laser cut in a circular motion around the base of these now shrunken growths, and then remove them by hand. Then find the right color laser tube to promote the growth of healthy cells there and see the whole area heal up and look exactly like the surrounding healthy tissue. After the normal cells are stimulated and healing takes place, leave your body via the route by which you entered. Once outside your body, breathe out and open your eyes.[45]

This visualization of color and images conveyed the needed instruction to the subconscious mind, which then brought about the inner surgery.

In summary, application of the fourth-ray formula involves four steps. As indicated by the first and second sentences, the first step is diagnosing the discordant condition, the second step is determining the specific sounds or colors that can be helpful, and the third step is determining how those sounds or colors can be applied in an effective way. As indicated by the third, fourth, and fifth sentences of the formula, there are five basic areas of application for this approach to healing: unifying a group of human beings; training or conditioning the emotional body of a patient who needs to receive treatment through some other means; preparing the consciousness of a dying person; directly bringing about physical or emotional healing; and removing diseased tissue. The fourth and final step is actually conveying the appropriate sounds or colors for one of these five areas, which completes the process ("And thus the work is done").

---

[45] G. Epstein, M.D., *Healing Visualizations: Creating Health with Imagery* (New York: Bantam Books, 1989), pp. 162, 163.

Ray Five

That which has been given must be used; that which emerges from within the given mode will find its place within the healer's plan. That which is hidden must be seen and from the three, great knowledge will emerge. For these the healer seeks. To these the healer adds the two which are as one, and so the fifth must play its part and the five must play its part and the five must function as if one. The energies descend, pass through and disappear, leaving the one who could respond with karma yet to dissipate and taking with them him who may not thus respond and so must likewise disappear.[46]

The name of the fifth ray is science or concrete knowledge, and the basic quality is discrimination. Because the fifth-ray formula describes a general theory of education, we shall refer to the healer as the teacher and the recipient as the student. This theory of education is applicable to teachers and students at all grade levels, and it describes how to select the curriculum and convey concrete knowledge in an effective way.

Effective education must include two kinds of efforts. The first is giving knowledge to students in the form of facts and information ("That which has been given"). The second is encouraging them to use their accumulated knowledge so that they have practical experience and grow in understanding ("must be used"). Thus, effective education is more than mere memory training, which was the emphasis of past educational methods. It also indicates goals that students can achieve through their endeavors and promises further enlightenment for those who attain the goals.[47]

---

[46] Bailey, *Esoteric Healing*, p. 710.
[47] A. A. Bailey, *Education in the New Age* (1954; reprint; New York: Lucis Publishing Company, 1974), pp. 1, 3, 82.

Achieving further enlightenment is equivalent to building an additional link between the various parts or vehicles of the inner human constitution. Because human beings integrate their inner vehicles in a particular order, the curriculum ought to reflect the same order. In this way, the students have the capacity to apply the information that they receive and are helped in achieving the next stage in their integration. The teacher needs to discern the vehicle where a given student's attention is primarily centered or focussed and then instruct the student in such a manner that a shift of that focus into the next higher vehicle becomes possible. In other words, the vehicle that seems to be of primary importance can and should become of secondary importance as it becomes simply the instrument of what is higher than itself. When the center of the student's consciousness emerges from within the next higher vehicle, then he or she will be ready to receive the next segment within the teacher's curriculum ("that which emerges from within the given mode will find its place within the healer's plan").

For instance, if the physical body is the center of the student's life, then the objective of the educational process is to awaken the emotional nature. If the emotional body is the center, the objective is to make the concrete mind the dominating factor. If the concrete mind is the center, the objective is to bring the soul activity into fuller expression. Thus, progress is made from step to step until the top of the ladder is reached.[48]

When students have mastered a segment within the curriculum—which means that they have shifted the focus of their attention into their next higher vehicle—that mastery must be apparent in their physical behavior ("That which is hidden must be seen"). Initially, there may be a conflict between their old and new ways of acting in the physical world, but eventually there must be a tangible demonstration of their higher integration. For instance, they may have different interests, be more effective or creative in their work, or have different kinds of

---

[48] Bailey, *Education in the New Age*, pp. 6, 7.

companions. Thus, the matriculation of students need not be based on competitive examinations, which generally only test whether they have memorized imparted knowledge. Their own lives will demonstrate whether they are ready to pass on to a higher grade.

Any segment within the curriculum should consist of appropriate and balanced instruction regarding the physical, emotional, and mental worlds ("the three"). For instance, for those who are unfolding the concrete mind, the imparted knowledge might include information regarding diet and exercise, methods for overcoming negative emotions, and the values and ideals found in history and literature. For those who are unfolding the soul nature, the knowledge might include breathing exercises, visualization techniques that release the power of the imagination, and instruction in receptive medi- tation. The purpose of receptive meditation is to align the con- crete mind with the soul, both of which belong to the mental plane or world.[49]

When the knowledge is initially imparted, it is only sec- ondhand from the point of view of the students because they have yet to see the truth of it for themselves. Thus, the students need to experiment with that knowledge: implement the sci- entific method, utilize tests, eliminate what is false, isolate those aspects requiring further investigation, and apply what they understand to be truth in their personal lives. Through this process, they will gain both firsthand knowledge and wis- dom. Secondhand knowledge is theoretical and based on trust in the intelligence of others, but firsthand knowledge is proven and factual. Wisdom is an outgrowth of firsthand knowledge and is the power to understand the meaning that lies behind the observed facts plus the power to apply those facts in a practical way. Both firsthand knowledge and wisdom are the intelligent result of hard work, and they come from exper-

---

[49] Z. F. Lansdowne, *Rules for Spiritual Initiation* (York Beach, ME: Samuel Weiser, 1990), pp. 1-42.

iment and experience, from learning the meaning of both success and failure, and from the struggle to move forward into greater and clearer light. If the students take an experimental approach, then from out of the secondhand knowledge regarding the three worlds that is imparted to them, both firsthand knowledge and wisdom will emerge ("and from the three, great knowledge will emerge").[50]

The next portion of the formula gives the qualifications that teachers must meet in order to be effective. The third sentence describes the desired mastery for the emotional nature, and the fourth sentence describes it for the mental nature.

People who are inclined to be teachers often find satisfaction in the power of thought and take pride in their mental competence. For instance, they often are susceptible to the following glamours or emotional distortions: the glamour of the intellect, the glamour of knowledge and definition, and the glamour of assurance based on a narrow point of view. As a result, they may be tempted to organize their curriculum or to present their information as a way of demonstrating their own mental superiority. So-called metaphysicians often succumb to this type of temptation, with classes filled with exotic and unusual information but producing no tangible changes in the lives of the students. Thus, teachers must have sufficient control over their emotional nature to remain dedicated to a selfless purpose: the further enlightenment of their students ("For these the healer seeks").[51]

For instance, rather than giving well-formulated explanations, teachers might be more helpful if they merely raise questions, while dropping hints subtly into the students' minds. With this pedagogical approach, the students are encouraged to take an active role, awaken their intuitive faculty, and discover the

[50] Bailey, *Discipleship in the New Age*, vol. 2, pp. 393, 394; Bailey, *A Treatise on White Magic*, pp. 14, 15.

[51] A. A. Bailey, *Glamour: A World Problem* (1950; reprint; New York: Lucis Publishing Company, 1971), p. 122.

power to find their own answers for themselves. Teachers can persistently apply this approach only if they have overcome the egotistical desire to be admired and honored for their great learning.[52]

Let us consider the required mental attainment. In addition to having firsthand knowledge about the physical, emotional, and mental aspects of the curriculum, teachers must have wisdom regarding the application of the knowledge as well as insights into the students—which means perceiving their points of evolution and special needs. Wisdom and insight are two facets of the intuitive faculty ("To these the healer adds the two which are as one"). Thus, all elements of the fifth or mental plane must play their parts ("and so the fifth must play its part"): the concrete mind for knowledge, the soul for wisdom, and the spiritual mind for insights. Furthermore, the three types of knowledge, the wisdom, and the insights must work together in a coordinated way ("and the five must play its part"). In particular, the expression of concrete knowledge must be guided by wisdom, which in turn must be guided by insights ("and the five must function as if one").

The key to good education is not having any blockages to the natural free flow of knowledge. For any segment within the curriculum, the students initially receive the imparted knowledge on the mental level. However, constant reading and hearing of instructions, when not carried into action on the physical plane, are a way of escaping from reality. It is the way of drifting, of thinking but not working, of having the illusion of progress without the pain of accomplishment. To avoid blocking the knowledge, the students must meet it in an experimental way and discover how to apply it in their daily lives. Through this process, the knowledge eventually manifests or precipitates on the physical plane ("The energies descend"), which means that it molds the personal lives of the students.

---

[52] Bailey, *Education in the New Age*, p. 25.

Afterward, the knowledge passes through the students as more enlightened speech and activities, and then it is received by others out in the world ("pass through and disappear").[53]

Some teachers try to hold on to their students, pressuring them to remain loyal and obedient. Such teachers might be leaders of exploitative cults, people who gain prestige by having many followers, or founders of philosophical or psychological movements that compete with rival movements founded by other teachers. Because this separative spirit also blocks the free flow of knowledge, it should not be part of the educational process. If some students are able to learn more or wish to be of assistance, then they could stay with their teachers and dissipate further ignorance ("leaving the one who could respond with karma yet to dissipate"). But if other students have learned everything that they wish to learn, they ought to be free to leave and go their own way ("and taking with them him who may not thus respond and so must likewise disappear").

Ray Six

Cleaving the waters, let the power descend, the healer cries. He minds not how the waters may respond; they oft bring stormy waves and dire and dreadful happenings. The end is good. The trouble will be ended when the storm subsides and energy has fulfilled its charted destiny. Straight to the heart the power is forced to penetrate, and into every channel, nadi, nerve and spleen the power must seek a passage and a way and thus confront the enemy who has effected entrance and settled down to live. Ejection—ruthless,

---

[53] Bailey, *Discipleship in the New Age*, vol. 2, p. 39; Bailey, *Esoteric Psychology*, vol. 2, pp. 711, 712.

sudden and complete—is undertaken by the one who sees naught else but perfect functioning and brooks no interference. This perfect functioning opens thus the door to life eternal or to life on earth for yet a little while.[54]

The sixth ray is called the ray of devotion or idealism, and its basic quality is devoted sensitivity to an ideal. In the case of the sixth-ray formula, the ideal is self-healing, and devotion to that ideal is expressed through the system of medical treatment known as homeopathy. In this system, the objective is to find a substance that would cause, in a healthy person, symptoms similar to those a sick person is experiencing. When a match is made, that substance is given in very small, safe doses.

Samuel Hahnemann (1755-1843), a German physician, first coined the word *homeopathy* (*homoios* in Greek means "similar" and *pathos* means "suffering") and was the founder of this approach to medicine. At the time that he practiced, quinine was the standard remedy for treating malaria. By experimenting on himself, Hahnemann discovered that quinine caused him to have the prime symptoms of malaria including intermittent fevers. In other words, he discovered that the treatment for malaria induces the symptoms of malaria in a healthy person. As a result, Hahnemann came to the following conclusion: quinine is able to cure malaria because it creates an artificial illness within the body, similar to malaria, that stimulates the body's own defense mechanisms into action. After experimenting with other drugs, he formulated the principle that "like cures like," which means that a disorder is cured by a drug that produces effects in the body similar to the disorder.

Hahnemann also coined the word *allopathy* (*allos* in Greek means "other"), and he used this word to refer to the treatment of disease by using remedies that produce effects different from or opposite to those produced by the disease. In other

---

[54] Bailey, *Esoteric Healing*, p. 711.

words, allopathy proceeds on the principle of administering substances that remove or alleviate the patient's symptoms. Unfortunately, this type of remedy may not have any effect on the underlying condition that produced those symptoms and it may create unwanted side-effects. For instance, morphine (a derivative of opium) is an allopathic drug that can remove the pain of cancer, but it will not cure the illness and may result in addiction.

In modern usage, the word *allopathy* is ambiguous because it could refer to the original meaning given by Hahnemann, in which case it would denote treatment that was the direct opposite of homeopathy, or it could refer simply to the orthodox science of medicine as practiced today. As an example of the latter usage, *The American Medical Association Encyclopedia of Medicine* defines allopathy as a "term that describes conventional medicine as practiced by a graduate of a medical school or college granting the MD degree."[55] These two meanings for allopathy are not the same because modern orthodox medicine includes remedies that are based on the homeopathic principle. One example is allergy treatment, which uses small doses of allergens to create an antibody response. Other examples are radiation to treat cancer (radiation causes cancer), salt used within oral rehydration therapy (salt causes thirst), digitalis for heart conditions (digitalis creates heart conditions), and ritalin for hyperactive children (ritalin creates hyperactivity). On the other hand, orthodox medicine employs a large number of antibiotics, tranquilizers, sleeping medications, laxatives, antidepressants, and antihistamines that are allopathic in their application according to Hahnemann's original meaning. The descriptive names for these drugs, often with the prefix *anti-*, show the principle on which they are prescribed.[56]

---

[55] C. B. Clayman, ed., *The American Medical Association Encyclopedia of Medicine* (New York: Random House, 1989).

[56] D. Ullman, *Homeopathy: Medicine for the 21st Century* (Berkeley, CA: North Atlantic Books, 1988), p. 6; M. Weiner and K. Goss, *The Complete Book of Homeopathy* (Garden City, NY: Avery Publishing Group, 1989), p. 6.

The first sentence of the sixth formula describes how a homeopathic remedy is prepared. The original medicinal substance is subjected to a process of serial dilution in the following manner. One part by volume of the original substance is diluted with 99 parts of distilled water or ethyl alcohol, which then is vigorously shaken. One part of this solution is diluted further with 99 parts of distilled water or ethyl alcohol and then shaken again. Through additional dilutions ("Cleaving the waters"), the proportion of the original substance still present in the solution can be reduced to any desired level ("let the power descend"). If the dosage is too large, then the patient would experience a severe aggravation of symptoms. One of the accepted principles of homeopathy is that the proper dose is the minimum amount needed to stimulate a cure, which is the minimum amount needed to produce a slight aggravation of symptoms. Thus, the physician experiments with differing numbers of dilutions until he or she discovers the proper dose of the medicine ("the healer cries").[57]

How is a homeopathic remedy prescribed? When any drug is given to a healthy person, it actually produces two consecutive and opposite sets of symptoms, called the primary and secondary actions of the drug. For instance, if a drug causes a person to experience profound stupefied sleep (primary action), then the following night he or she will experience sleeplessness (secondary action). Or if it initially causes constipation (primary action), then later diarrhea will ensue (secondary action). A particular remedy is prescribed if it is the medicine whose primary action in a healthy person most closely matches the symptoms of the disease being treated. The secondary action is the evoked or reactive response of the self-curative power that lies within the person.[58]

The physician is not anxious about how the patient's bodily fluids may respond to the medication ("He minds not

---

[57] Weiner and Goss, *The Complete Book of Homeopathy*, p. 49.
[58] Weiner and Goss, *The Complete Book of Homeopathy*, pp. 35, 36.

how the waters may respond"). Because of the way the medication was prescribed, those fluids often respond by increasing the severity of various unpleasant symptoms such as fever, inflammation, cough, diarrhea, and mucus discharges ("they oft bring stormy waves and dire and dreadful happenings"). This increase in severity is called the "homeopathic aggravation." It is not only expected but *desirable* that an aggravation of symptoms be produced.[59]

Each symptom is actually an adaptive effort of the body to defend itself. For instance, fever usually accompanies bacterial or viral infection, and it helps to fight the infection by increasing the production of interferon (an antiviral agent) and by increasing the mobility and activity of white blood cells. Inflammation occurs when the body seeks to wall off, heat up, and burn out infective agents or foreign matter. Coughing helps to clear breathing passages. Diarrhea is a defensive effort of the body to remove pathogens or irritants more quickly from the colon. And mucus discharges are another way that the body gets rid of diseased material.[60]

Although the homeopathic remedy may temporarily increase the severity of the patient's symptoms, it also evokes into activity the self-curative power that lies within the patient ("The end is good"). The illness will be over when the body no longer needs to create symptoms for defending itself and when the evoked curative power has fulfilled its instinctive purpose ("The trouble will be ended when the storm subsides and energy has fulfilled its charted destiny").

The fifth sentence describes the effect of the remedy on a physiological level. The remedy is administered in such a way that it can be readily absorbed by the blood system. In practice, a homeopathic remedy is often given on lactose or sugar tablets, which then can dissolve on the tongue or be swal-

---

[59] G. Vithoulkas, *The Science of Homeopathy* (New York: Grove Press, 1980), pp. 227-229.
[60] Ullman, *Homeopathy: Medicine for the 21st Century*, pp. 4, 5.

lowed. After being absorbed by the blood system, the remedy is forced to move through the veins directly into the heart ("Straight to the heart the power is forced to penetrate"). After reaching the heart, the remedy is carried by the blood into every artery, capillary, nervous system, and organ ("and into every channel, nadi, nerve and spleen the power must seek a passage and a way"). The remedy was prescribed because it had the power to evoke the appropriate curative reactions. Those reactions can now occur throughout the body and thereby confront the illness wherever the latter has entered and is feeding on the body's vitality ("and thus confront the enemy who has effected entrance and settled down to live").

In the fourth-ray section of this chapter, we introduced the concept of the subconscious mind. Ejection of any disorder is undertaken by a subconscious mind that allows nothing else but the proper functioning of the defense mechanisms and tolerates no interference with those mechanisms ("Ejection—ruthless, sudden and complete—is undertaken by the one who sees naught else but perfect functioning and brooks no interference"). Thus, the presence of a lingering illness shows that the activity of the patient's subconscious mind has been distorted and blocked to some extent. The homeopathic remedy can be thought of as a catalyst that releases the curative power of the patient's subconscious mind, which can then operate through various defensive responses.

Depending on the patient, the proper functioning of the defense mechanisms has two possible effects. For a dying or terminal patient, this functioning facilitates the natural processes of death, minimizes the suffering, and permits full awareness of the transition to the after-death experience ("This perfect functioning opens thus the door to life eternal"). As a result, the patient has the opportunity of passing through the transition with awareness, dignity, serenity, comfort, and freedom.

Accordingly, the presence of severe pain in a dying person shows that the defense mechanisms are not working properly. In this case, a homeopathic remedy could be given to stimulate the defense mechanisms, which would have the effect of alleviating the pain while permitting the maximum degree of awareness that the patient can muster. In addition, "it is often said in homeopathic circles that giving [homeopathic] palliative remedies in terminal cases may well mercifully shorten the final days of the patient."[61] In contrast, modern hospitals often use methods that have the opposite effects: powerful narcotics and tranquilizers that put patients into drugged, stupefied conditions; and invasive techniques that artificially prolong their lives.

For a nonterminal patient, the proper functioning of the defense mechanisms restores health and opens the door to an active life on the physical plane for an additional amount of time ("or to life on earth for yet a little while"). If this functioning is deficient, then it can be strengthened and harmonized by an appropriate homeopathic remedy.

During the past two hundred years, the homeopathic and allopathic movements have seemed like religious cults— fighting, criticizing, and ridiculing each other's theories and methods. Practitioners of both systems have often been sectarian, aggressive, and narrowminded. A step forward would be to place all forms of medication, whether homeopathic or allopathic, on a strictly scientific basis by subjecting them to double-blind experiments. In such an experiment, neither the researchers nor the subjects of the experiment know which subjects are receiving the medication being tested and which are receiving a placebo. A few double-blind experiments for homeopathic remedies have been reported, and these have demonstrated the efficacy of the remedies. However, the vast majority of the remedies used by homeopathic practitioners have not yet received this type of test.[62]

It is important to acknowledge that there is an appropriate place for all effective forms of healing, whether homeopathic or allopathic, exoteric or esoteric, and physical or psychological. Although homeopathic remedies can be used to cure many types of illnesses, some cases require the immediate and cer-

---

[61] Vithoulkas, *The Science of Homeopathy*, pp. 259, 268.
[62] Ullman, *Homeopathy: Medicine for the 21st Century,* pp. 55-66.

tain relief of symptoms that is provided by allopathic drugs. Other cases can be addressed by simple nutrition and life-style changes, and still others require surgery. In a given situation, more than one type of treatment may be appropriate.

Ray Seven

Energy and force must meet each other and thus the work is done. Colour and sound in ordered sequence must meet and blend and thus the work of magic can proceed. Substance and spirit must evoke each other and, passing through the centre of the one who seeks to aid, produce the new and good. The healer energises thus with life the failing life, driving it forth or anchoring it yet more deeply in the place of destiny. All seven must be used and through the seven there must pass the energies the need requires, creating the new man who has for ever been and will for ever be, and either here or there.[63]

The name of the seventh ray is ceremonial order or magic. Its basic quality is magic—which in this context is the ability to produce the outer appearance of an inner reality. The seventh and final formula describes an application of magic— namely, how to work with a gemstone so that it embodies the healing nature of the soul.

Gemstones have been used for healing since antiquity. In the method described in this section, the goal is to reestablish the natural harmony of the chakras within the patient's etheric body, which will then bring health to the dense physical body. Even though this goal seems to be intrinsically esoteric in nature, the method itself is exoteric because a tangible object, a gemstone, is used as the intermediary between the healer and

---

[63] Bailey, *Esoteric Healing*, p. 712.

the patient. The underlying theory is basically the same as that used for one of the fourth-ray techniques considered earlier in this chapter, namely, that of using sounds with a specific frequency to bring about physical health.

Before interpreting the seventh formula, it may be helpful to provide some background information. Most gemstones are crystals, and a crystal is a homogeneous structure with a regular lattice of atoms. According to the science of crystallography, the crystalline form for any mineral falls into one of seven basic categories. Table 4 (on page 64) gives the names, descriptions, and examples of these categories. Each category is defined by the number of its axes and the angles at which these axes intersect. The various faces or planes of a crystal reflect the orderly geometric arrangements of the individual atoms. The size of a crystal depends on how often the internal pattern repeats itself, which in turn depends on the supply of available material and the room for growth. Because of the orderly structure, all atoms of a crystal can vibrate together in unison.

The etheric body extends outside the dense physical body, and the major chakras are part of that portion of the etheric body that lies outside. Bailey states that the crown chakra is "just above the top of the head"; the brow chakra is "just in front of the eyes and forehead"; and the five spinal chakras (throat, heart, solar plexus, sacral, and basic) are "found in the etheric counterpart of the spinal column," which lies behind the dense physical spine. In particular, these spinal centers are at least two inches away from the dense physical spine for an undeveloped person and are even further away for an average person.[64]

Each major chakra has its own natural rhythm, note, or frequency. Due to subtle inner causes, a major chakra may be forced to vibrate at a frequency different from its true natural frequency. The ensuing chakra frequency affects the rate of

---

[64] A. A. Bailey, *Telepathy and the Etheric Vehicle* (1950; reprint; New York: Lucis Publishing Company, 1975), p. 146; Bailey, *Esoteric Healing*, p. 461.

Table 4. The Seven Crystal Systems.*

Crystal System	Description	Examples
Cubic or Isometric	Three equal axes intersect at right angles.	Diamond Garnet Lapis Lazuli Spinel
Hexagonal	Three equal axes are arranged at 120 degree angles in one plane and the main axis is at right angles to these, with a six-sided prism base.	Aquamarine Beryl Emerald Morganite Zincite
Tetragonal	Two axes of equal length and the third axis unequal, all being at right angles to each other.	Anatase Apophyllite Leucite Rutile Zircon
Orthorhombic	Three axes with different lengths are at right angles to each other.	Chrysoberyl Iolite Peridot Topaz
Monoclinic	Three unequal axes, two of which are at right angles to each other and the third is inclined.	Azurite Jadeite Kunzite Malachite Moonstone
Triclinic	Three unequal axes are inclined to each other.	Amazonite Rhodonite Turquoise
Trigonal or Rhombohedral	Same as the hexagonal system, except that the prism base is three-sided.	Agate Amethyst Jasper Quartz Ruby Sapphire

*Source: W. Schumann, Gemstones of the World (1977; reprint; New York: Sterling, 1986), pp. 18, 19.

bodily vibratory activity, the endocrine glands, the nervous system, and the responsiveness of the dense physical body to bacterial and viral infections. For instance, if the frequency of a chakra is too slow, then congestion occurs in the etheric body, which may produce distress in the dense physical body (such as congestion in the lungs). On the other hand, if the frequency of a chakra is too high, then the person may experience nervous disorders or have migraine headaches. According to Bailey, healers can develop the sense of touch in their hands and fingers that would enable them to ascertain the rate of vibration in any chakra.[65]

With this information, an interpretation of the seventh formula is possible. In the therapeutic application of gemstones, the first step is identifying the chakra in the patient's etheric body that governs the area of physical illness. When etheric energy with the right frequency and potency is applied to this chakra, the energy must interact with the internal forces of the chakra and cause the chakra to return to its true natural frequency ("Energy and force must meet each other"). The right rhythm and balance in the etheric body then brings health to the dense physical body ("and thus the work is done").

For instance, if the patient's disease is related to the stomach or liver, then the solar plexus chakra is treated. If the patient is suffering from difficulty with the heart or lungs, then the heart chakra is treated. If the patient is suffering from diseases of the bronchial tract, the throat, the mouth, or the ears, then the throat chakra is treated.[66]

The second step is selecting a gemstone that can vibrate sympathetically with the etheric energy that needs to be applied. When this gemstone is struck by the etheric energy, the stone must vibrate at the same frequency as the energy and augment it ("Colour and sound in ordered sequence must meet and blend"). The vibrational properties of a gemstone depend on the crystalline structure (as listed in Table 4 on page 64) and the type of atoms forming that structure. Some substances can vibrate sympathetically at more than one frequency. A good

---

[65] Bailey, *Esoteric Healing*, pp. 74-88.
[66] Bailey, *Esoteric Healing*, p. 602.

example is our tympanic membrane (ear drum), which can respond to any sound within the human range of hearing. If a gemstone can vibrate sympathetically at more than one frequency, then it might be suitable for treating more than one chakra. After selecting an appropriate gemstone, the healer can use that stone as a healing talisman in the step that follows ("and thus the work of magic can proceed").

An oscillator is any object that moves in a periodic manner. When energy passes between two oscillators having the same natural frequency, the two oscillators constitute what is called a *resonant system*. As an example, suppose that two tuning forks with the same pitch (that is, designed to vibrate at the same frequency) are located in a room. If we strike one tuning fork, then acoustic energy from that fork will move to the second fork and cause it to sound. Next, acoustic energy from the second fork will move back and reinforce the vibrations of the first one. Thus, energy will pass between the two forks in both directions. Another example of a resonant system is provided by the two violins discussed earlier in the fourth-ray section.

The third step is transferring etheric energy between the patient's chakra and the corresponding chakra of the healer. Because these two chakras have the same natural frequency, they can form a resonant system. The potency of the healer's chakra must be sufficient to evoke a response from the patient's chakra, which will then reinforce the vibrations in the healer's chakra ("Substance and spirit must evoke each other"). As Bailey describes the process, the healer's chakra "acts like a magnet, drawing forth a definite radiation from the patient."[67] The healer can facilitate these transfers by placing or holding the selected gemstone near the patient's chakra, enabling the energies to pass through the stone ("passing through the centre of the one who seeks to aid"). Depending on the type of gemstone that is used, the stone might amplify, purify, or both amplify and purify the energies.[68] When the resonant system is established,

---

[67] Bailey, *Esoteric Healing,* p. 604.

it will produce a new and better vibrational pattern in the patient's chakra ("produce the new and good").

Through accomplishing these steps, the healer uses the vital forces in his or her etheric body to harmonize the failing forces in the patient's etheric body ("The healer energises thus with life the failing life"). An interplay is established on etheric levels, and the energies of the two synchronized chakras are in rapport. The sole remaining task of the healer is to hold the situation steady, give the patient confidence, and encourage a period of waiting. During this period, the resonant system drives out surplus energy from the patient's chakra if that chakra is overstimulated; or it augments the energy if that chakra is depleted ("driving it forth or anchoring it yet more deeply in the plane of destiny"). As a result, steady and normal activity occurs in the patient's chakra that controls the area of disease.[69]

The last sentence of the formula describes three prerequisites that the healer should meet before being ready to practice this type of healing. The first one is having adequate technical knowledge regarding the chakras. The diagnosis of any given patient involves determining the chakra or chakras that need to be treated. A working knowledge about all seven major chakras must be used to obtain valid diagnoses for the full range of possible illnesses ("All seven must be used").

Second, the healer ought to possess at least one gemstone that is appropriate for treating each chakra. Seven stones, one for each major chakra, are sufficient for transmitting all healing energies that any patient might require ("and through the seven there must pass the energies the need requires").

The third prerequisite is aligning the personality with the soul ("creating the new man who has for ever been and will for ever be") and expressing this heightened consciousness through both the crown chakra and the appropriate

---

[68] W. Richardson and L. Huett, *Spiritual Value of Gem Stones* (Marina del Rey, CA: DeVorss, 1980), pp. 15, 42, 62, 91; Bailey, *Esoteric Healing*, p. 370.
[69] Bailey, *Esoteric Healing*, p. 605.

ness through both the crown chakra and the appropriate lower chakra ("and either here or there"). It must be remembered that the soul is the vehicle for abstract thought. When alignment with the soul is achieved, an abstract understanding of how to work with gemstones—which is a seventh-ray ability—can pass from the soul to the crown chakra. Afterwards, the healer holds his or her consciousness steady in the crown chakra with the "eye of direction" turned to the needed center, which is the one that corresponds to the chakra being treated in the patient. Then by the power of thought, under the agency of the will, the healer stimulates the needed center so that it radiates etheric energy with the right frequency and potency to the patient.[70]

In this discussion concerning the seventh-ray method of exoteric healing, the main omissions are the associations between gemstones and chakras. Bailey did not provide any information of that type in her books, but several writers of more recent books do offer such associations. For instance, Wallace Richardson and Lenora Huett relate each of the seven crystal classes listed in Table 4 (on page 64) to one of the seven major chakras.[71] Other writers relate one or more gemstones to each major chakra.[72] Unfortunately, these writers often contradict each other because very few (if any) obtained their information through scientific or empirical investigations. Instead, they generally received their data through psychic mediumship or what is sometimes called "channeling." However, mediumship is notoriously unreliable. If the mediums are

---

[70] Bailey, *Glamour, A World Problem*, pp. 251-253; Bailey, *Esoteric Healing*, pp. 602-607.

[71] Richardson and Huett, *Spiritual Value of Gem Stones*, pp. 20-23.

[72] D. Maerz and D. Maerz, "Crystal Spectrum," in *The Crystal Sourcebook*, J. V. Milewski and V. L. Harford, eds. (Santa Fe, NM: Mystic Crystal Publications, 1988), pp. 297-303; P .L. Chase and J. Pawlik, *The Newcastle Guide To Healing With Gemstones* (North Hollywood CA: Newcastle Publishing Company, 1989), pp. 57-155.

involved with trance conditions or have not confronted their own glamours and illusions, then they may be deceived regarding the source of their data and they may deceive others.

If there is any practical value in using a particular gemstone as part of a healing method, then it must be possible to confirm that value through a controlled scientific experiment. For instance, Leonard Laskow, an obstetrician-gynecologist, conducted two series of clinical trials to test the value of using quartz crystal when treating herpes. The first group of patients was treated with medical technology (a device called an electroacuscope), and the second group was treated by focusing healing energy through a quartz crystal. Laskow observed a substantial decrease in the duration, frequency, and intensity of herpetic lesions within both groups of patients.[73] Other medical doctors have also experimented with gemstones and demonstrated their value.[74] Nevertheless, much more empirical research needs to be done.

---

[73] L. Laskow, M.D., "Transformational Medicine," in *The Crystal Sourcebook*, pp. 116-126.
[74] L. Badgley, M.D., "Crystal Diagnosis and Therapy," in *The Crystal Sourcebook*, pp. 134-142; J. J. Adams, M.D., "Energy Medicine," in *The Crystal Sourcebook*, pp. 143-148.

Chapter 3

Methods of Service

*The responsibility of the great states is to serve
and not to dominate the world.*
—Harry S. Truman

Because this chapter emphasizes the ray of the soul (or soul ray), this concept needs to be examined in more detail. The fundamental premise is that the soul of each human being primarily expresses the particular quality denoted by the soul ray, which could be any one of the seven rays. Through its quality, the soul ray affects the nature of the mental, emotional, and physical bodies, predisposes us to certain strengths and weaknesses, and affects our relationships with other human beings. If we are on the path of probation or discipleship, our effort is to integrate personality with soul. Because this effort of integration is intuitively guided by the soul, there are seven basic processes of integration, one for each type of soul ray. As a result, our soul ray determines our method of working on these paths, and it also indicates our destiny in the sense of predisposing us to certain activities.[1]

If we have begun the process of integrating personality with soul, then knowledge of our soul ray would be valuable

---

[1] A. A. Bailey, *Esoteric Psychology*, vol. 1 (1936; reprint; New York: Lucis Publishing Company, 1975), pp. 401-403.

because it can help explain and clarify our experiences. By carefully examining the various facets of our lives, we should be able to discern which of the seven rays is our particular soul ray. For instance, our soul ray affects our virtues and vices, inner conflicts, aspirations, hobbies, glamours, approach to the spiritual path, method of meditation, and career. Several earlier books on the seven rays discussed alternative ways of identifying the soul ray and gave examples of well-known historical figures who illustrated each type of soul ray.[2]

Chapter 2 viewed the human soul as having seven different qualities that correspond to the seven rays. The present chapter will still refer to those qualities but will consider them as subrays of the soul ray. These subrays could be thought of as seven different shades of the same underlying quality. For instance, one person might have a first-ray soul and another might have a fifth-ray soul. If both persons express the third-ray quality of their souls, then the first person would actually express the third subray of the first soul ray and the second person would express the third subray of the fifth soul ray. Because there are seven soul rays and because each soul ray consists of seven subrays, there are forty-nine different soul qualities.

For each soul ray, Table 5 (on page 73) gives the ray name plus six characteristic qualities that were previously tabulated by Bailey. Each quality describes how the soul ray is expressed through a subray that corresponds to another soul ray. Each soul ray also has a seventh characteristic quality that is denoted by the ray name and is not specifically stated in the six listed qualities. This seventh quality is the synthesis of the listed qualities, and it represents the subray that corresponds to the soul ray. The order of the qualities in the table is the same as the order in which they are discussed in this chapter.

It is important to emphasize that the actual qualities that we display depend on our point of evolution. Because the qualities listed in Table 5 (on page 73) are characteristics of

---

[2] M. D. Robbins, Ph.D., *Tapestry of the Gods* (Jersey City Heights, NJ: University of the Seven Rays Publishing House, 1988); Z. F. Lansdowne, *The Rays and Esoteric Psychology* (York Beach, ME: Samuel Weiser, 1989).

Table 5. Characteristic Qualities for the Seven Soul Rays.*

Ray	Name	Qualities
One	Will or Power	Singleness of purpose Dynamic power Clear vision Detachment Solitariness Sense of time
Two	Love-Wisdom	Love divine Attraction Radiance Power to save Expansion or inclusiveness Wisdom
Three	Active Intelligence or Adaptability	Mental illumination Power to manifest Scientific investigation Power to evolve Balance Power to produce synthesis on the physical plane
Four	Harmony through Conflict	Power to penetrate the depths of matter Harmony of the spheres Synthesis of true beauty Dual aspects of desire Power to express divinity Power to reveal the path
Five	Concrete Knowledge or Science	Emergence into form and out of form Power to make the Voice of the Silence heard Manifestation of the great white light Revelation of the way Initiating activity Purification with fire

Table 5. Characteristic Qualities for the Seven Soul Rays (cont.).*

Ray	Name	Qualities
Six	Devotion or Idealism	Overcoming the waters of the emotional nature Endurance and fearlessness Power to kill out desire Self-immolation Spurning that which is not desired Power to detach oneself
Seven	Ceremonial Order or Magic	Power to create Power to think Mental power Power to vivify Power to cooperate Revelation of the beauty of God

*Source: A. A. Bailey, *Esoteric Psychology,* vol. 1 (1936; reprint; New York: Lucis Publishing Company, 1975), pp. 63-87.

the soul, we can display them only if we are starting to become integrated with the soul and live as the soul. But if we are still focussed in the personality and living as the personality, then our characteristics could be the direct opposite of the ones listed in this table.

If we study with care the six qualities listed for each ray, we may find an indication as to which ray is our own soul ray. Do the various qualities for a particular ray evoke our intuitive understanding so that we recognize ourselves? Perhaps we can see our life tendencies and purpose, or our latent and deeply desired spiritual nature. If we believe that a particular ray is our soul ray, then the associated qualities will show what we have to do, what we have to express, and what we have to overcome. Thus, if we apply this chapter in the right way, it will be profitable and useful in our experience.

Each of Bailey's symbolic formulas has three levels of significance. In the level considered in this chapter, each formula describes how people with the corresponding soul ray might display the qualities listed in Table 5 (on page 73) when they are providing service to the world. The underlying assumption is that these people have already achieved advanced positions on the path of discipleship and so have developed the capacity to express the characteristic qualities of their souls.

Ray One

Let the dynamic force which rules the hearts of all within Shamballa come to my aid, for I am worthy of that aid. Let it descend unto the third, pass to the fifth and focus on the seventh. These words mean not what doth at sight appear. The third, the fifth, the seventh lie within the first and come from out the Central Sun of spiritual livingness. The highest then awakens within the one who knows and within the one who must be healed and thus the two are one. This is mystery deep. The blending of the healing force effects the work desired; it may bring death, that great release, and re-establish thus the fifth, the third, the first, but not the seventh.[3]

Let us consider what the term *Shamballa* denotes in esoteric philosophy, which is different from the mythical interpretation used in chapter 2. An important principle is "As above, so below," which means that the macrocosm resembles the microcosm. In applying this principle, think of the microcosm as being the life of a human being and the macrocosm as being the life of our planet. Just as a human being has seven centers of energy

---

[3] A. A. Bailey, *Esoteric Healing* (1953; reprint; New York: Lucis Publishing Company, 1978), pp. 706, 707.

called chakras, the planetary life has analogous centers of energy. In esoteric philosophy, Shamballa is "the center where the Will of God is known," and it consists of a council of advanced beings who collectively constitute the planetary crown or head chakra. These beings are the product of past evolutionary systems and have long ago passed through the human stage of experience. Just as the human crown chakra is the receptive, focalizing, and distributing agent of the spiritual will for the etheric body, Shamballa is the corresponding agent for our planet.[4]

The first three methods in this chapter are more advanced versions of the corresponding ones described in the preceding chapter. The first method in chapter 2 began with the invocation of goodwill from the soul. In this chapter, the first method begins with the invocation of the spiritual will from the spiritual triad, and the entire method shows how first-ray people (that is, people having the first ray as their soul ray) might display their characteristic qualities listed in Table 5 (on page 73).

1. *Singleness of purpose.* Advanced first-ray servers are able to invoke and receive the spiritual will, which is the force that rules all within the esoteric center known as Shamballa ("Let the dynamic force which rules the hearts of all within Shamballa come to my aid"). The spiritual will comes from the atmic plane, passes through the soul, and reaches the crown chakra, where it is experienced as the dynamic purpose of serving the divine plan. The expression of power on the physical plane depends on singleness of purpose. Because advanced servers have previously removed such impediments as pride, ambition, arrogance, and the desire to control others ("for I am worthy of that aid"), they are able to maintain the spiritual will as the single purpose within their consciousness.[5]

---

[4] A. A. Bailey, *Telepathy and the Etheric Vehicle* (1950; reprint; New York: Lucis Publishing Company, 1975), pp. 183, 190; A. A. Bailey, *Discipleship in the New Age*, vol. 2 (1955; reprint; New York: Lucis Publishing Company, 1972), pp. 159, 519, 520.

[5] A. A. Bailey, *A Treatise on White Magic* (1934; reprint; New York: Lucis Publishing Company, 1974), p. 558.

2. *Dynamic power.* The third eye is formed by the synthesis, or vibratory interaction, between the forces of the soul working through the crown chakra and the forces of the personality working through the brow chakra, and it takes the semblance of an eye looking out between the two dense physical eyes. By focussing and directing the spiritual will, the third eye can bring the lower five chakras under rhythmic control. In this process, the spiritual will descends into the third or throat chakra, passes through each intermediate chakra, and reaches the seventh or basic chakra ("Let it descend unto the third, pass to the fifth and focus on the seventh"). Although these words seem to suggest that the spiritual will is a discrete package of force that passes from one chakra to another, that is not the case ("These words mean not what doth at sight appear"). One uses the third eye to contemplate one's lower nature, implying that the lower five chakras lie within a steady ray of spiritual will. In this context, a *ray* is defined as an emanation that is continuous in essence with its source. Because the lower five chakras lie within a steady emanation that extends back to the third eye, they are impelled by the dynamic purpose coming from there ("The third, the fifth, the seventh lie within the first and come from out the Central Sun of spiritual livingness"). As a result, one gains the dynamic power to express the spiritual will through the thoughts, feelings, and actions of the personality.[6]

3. *Clear vision.* After the spiritual will is imposed over the lower nature, the highest capacity awakens within each of the personality vehicles. First of all, clear vision awakens within the mental body, which is the instrument for expressing knowledge ("The highest then awakens within the one who knows"). By having clear vision, first-ray servers know when to use the energy of desire and take the next step in service. Afterwards, seeing that they have fulfilled their part, they know when to relinquish their emotional involvement, enabling them to pass on without experiencing pride over what they have done

---

[6] Bailey, *A Treatise on White Magic,* pp. 212-214; Bailey, *Esoteric Healing,* p. 604; A. A. Bailey, *Glamour: A World Problem* (1950; reprint; New York: Lucis Publishing Company, 1971), pp. 250-252.

or depression because of any lack of accomplishment. Through this process, they can give all they have in selfless service and then achieve true humility by forgetting that they have given of themselves.[7]

4. *Detachment*: The emotional body acts in its highest capacity only when it acts without attachment to persons, places, or things. By living in this world, however, people acquire emotional attachments that must be eliminated before they can render true service. After clear vision awakens in the mind, detachment then awakens in the emotional body ("and within the one who must be healed"). The mind brings about this emotional healing by understanding the origin and meaning of attachment rather than by hating or suppressing it. After becoming detached, one is ready to lead and help one's followers and to learn who those followers are.

5. *Solitariness*: When clear vision and detachment are awakened, there is solitariness in the sense that the spiritual will is united with and expressed through the personality ("and thus the two are one"). The characteristic of solitariness also has some deeper meanings ("This is mystery deep"). By cultivating inner detachment, one can merge oneself in the consciousness of someone else and thereby ascertain the best way to help and stimulate that person to renewed self-effort. One can also experience the stage of consciousness known as "isolated unity." Here, one sees the whole as a single entity and regards oneself, not theoretically but as a realized fact, as having the identity of the whole. This whole is that complete organism of which one can feel and know oneself to be a part; it is something that is progressively realized and could be a group, environment, nation, or the entire human kingdom of nature. The whole is "isolated" in one's consciousness, and the word "unity" indicates one's relationship to the whole.[8]

---

[7] A. A. Bailey, *Discipleship in the New Age*, vol. 1 (1944; reprint; New York: Lucis Publishing Company, 1976), p. 417.

[8] Bailey, *Discipleship in the New Age*, vol. 1, pp. 416, 417; A. A. Bailey, *Esoteric Psychology*, vol. 2 (1942; reprint; New York: Lucis Publishing Company, 1975), pp. 391, 392.

6. *Sense of time.* The blending of the spiritual will with the personality accomplishes the desired service ("The blending of the healing force effects the work desired"), which may be death and destruction ("it may bring death"). The word *form* is a general term that can refer to many kinds of structures, such as a religious organizations, educational systems, political parties, and social customs. After a particular form is built, that form is used for as long as possible. Eventually the time comes when the form no longer serves the indwelling life, when the structure atrophies and becomes vulnerable. By having clear vision, first-ray servers sense the appropriate time when an outmoded form ought to be destroyed in order for evolutionary growth to occur. They then destroy that form, which releases the door of opportunity for the potential builders of a new and better form ("that great release").

Afterwards, the potential builders establish a planning process to reconsider and reformulate their response to human needs ("and re-establish thus"). They ideally use the fifth subray of their soul rays for examining their motives, the third subray for devising new plans, and the first subray for developing new goals or governing principles ("the fifth, the third, the first"). They should not use the seventh subray for constructing a new form ("but not the seventh") until they have been patient and understand clearly what to do.

Ray Two

Let the healing energy descend, carrying its dual lines of life and its magnetic force. Let that magnetic living force withdraw and supplement that which is present in the seventh, opposing four and six to three and seven, but dealing not with five. The circular, inclusive vortex—descending to the point— disturbs, removes and then supplies and thus the work is done.

The heart revolves; two hearts revolve as one; the
twelve within the vehicle, the twelve within the head
and the twelve upon the plane of soul endeavor,
cooperate as one and thus the work is done. Two
energies achieve this consummation and the three
whose number is a twelve respond to the greater
twelve. The life is known and the years prolonged.[9]

According to the doctrine of hylozoism, all matter is
endowed with life. Any form is constructed out of infinitesi-
mal lives, which in their totality constitute a composite life, and
each composite life in its turn is a corporate part of a still greater
life. For instance, each atom in your physical body is ensouled
by an elemental life. Your physical body is a composite life that
incorporates the lives of the individual atoms, and your body
is ensouled by you. Our planet can also be viewed as a composite life that incorporates the lives of all forms that exist on
our planet. In theosophy, the informing, ensouling life of our
planet is called the *planetary Logos*. Thus, the planetary Logos
is the One in Whom we live and move and have our being, Whose
life integrates the planet as a whole, and Whose life pours through
all forms—great or small—that in their aggregate constitute
the planetary form. Furthermore, our solar system can also be
viewed as a composite life that incorporates the lives of all plan-
ets in the system. In theosophy, the informing, ensouling life
of our solar system is called the *solar Logos*.[10]

As discussed in the second section of chapter 2, the number *twelve* can represent the concept of heart on different levels. For instance, a twelve-petalled lotus can symbolize either
the heart chakra or the soul, the latter being the heart center
of the inner human constitution. On the macrocosmic scale,
Bailey indicates that a twelve-petalled lotus can also symbolize

[9] Bailey, *Esoteric Healing,* pp. 707, 708.
[10] A. A. Bailey, *A Treatise on Cosmic Fire* (1925; reprint; New York: Lucis
Publishing Company, 1977), p. 638; Bailey, *Telepathy and the Etheric Vehicle,*
pp. 182, 183; Bailey, *Esoteric Psychology,* vol. 1, pp. 149-152.

either the heart center of the planetary Logos or the heart center of the solar Logos. The latter is sometimes called the *heart of the sun*.[11]

Because a plane on the microcosmic scale is the same as a subplane on the macrocosmic scale, the seven planes illustrated in figure 1 (on page 3) constitute only the macrocosmic physical plane. Just as the human heart chakra is located on the etheric subplanes, the heart center of the planetary Logos is located on the fourth macrocosmic etheric plane, which is our buddhic plane. Just as the human soul is located on the mental plane, the heart center of the solar Logos resides on the macrocosmic mental plane. Thus, our heart chakra and soul correspond to the heart centers of the planetary Logos and solar Logos, respectively, on the macrocosmic scale.[12]

The second method of both the preceding and present chapters is concerned with counseling. In the preceding chapter, a counselor is able to be insightful by receiving inspiration from an incorporeal spirit guide. The present chapter considers a second-ray counselor who is in a more advanced position. Here, a counselor is able to be insightful by displaying the characteristic qualities of the soul.

1. *Love divine.* Spiritual love is the intuition that God is present within all bodily forms, and it is the source of both compassion and positive regard. Compassion, as the word is being used here, is the intuition of the essential nonseparateness and unity of human beings; whereas positive regard is a feeling of acceptance, appreciation, and respect for another person. Compassion relates to humanity as a whole, whereas positive regard relates to another person. After achieving sufficient integration with their own souls, second-ray counselors are able to invoke and receive spiritual love, carrying both compassion and positive regard into their awareness ("Let the healing energy descend, carrying its dual lines of life").

---

[11] A. A. Bailey, *Esoteric Astrology* (1951; reprint; New York: Lucis Publishing Company, 1979), p. 47

[12] Bailey, *Esoteric Astrology,* pp. 47, 594.

2. *Attraction*: When the counselors receive spiritual love, their experience of it is sensed by others. They refrain from separative activities such as criticism and off-putting remarks. Their affirming and supportive nature makes them attractive—capable of drawing or magnetizing to themselves those people whom they can instruct or aid ("and its magnetic force").

3. *Radiance*: Compassion and positive regard can radiate from a counselor's etheric body and help other individuals who are present on the seventh or physical plane ("Let that magnetic living force withdraw and supplement that which is present in the seventh"). In particular, compassion can radiate via the heart chakra and positive regard via the solar plexus chakra. This radiance helps the recipients in removing or opposing two separations: between the unifying love of the fourth or buddhic plane and their emotional bodies on the sixth or emotional plane ("opposing four and six"); and between the impersonal or altruistic motives of the third or atmic plane and their behavior on the seventh or physical plane ("to three and seven"). But this radiance does not help them to strengthen or clarify their concrete minds, which are on the fifth or mental plane ("but dealing not with five"). As we shall discuss in chapter 4, the latter can be accomplished by radiation that emanates from the throat chakra.[13]

4. *Power to save*: Criticism and resentment distort perception and block understanding, whereas positive regard allows for precise perception of the underlying thoughts. When the counselors have the feeling of positive regard, their minds act as searchlights that reveal the inner point of disturbance within each person who needs assistance ("The circular, inclusive vortex—descending to the point—disturbs"). After gaining this clarity, the counselors can speak words that have the power to remove the disturbance and supply harmony ("removes

---

[13] Bailey, *A Treatise on Cosmic Fire*, p. 863; Bailey, *Telepathy and the Etheric Vehicle*, pp. 8, 20.

and then supplies"). Nevertheless, people must save themselves through understanding the words spoken to them and through their self-initiated application of that understanding to their daily lives. Thus, the work of salvation is accomplished not by the words themselves, but by each person's reaction and response to the words ("and thus the work is done").[14]

5. *Expansion or inclusiveness:* Second-ray people have the inherent capacity of inclusive reason—which is the ability both to sense the greater whole and to grasp the meticulous detail of that whole—but this capacity is realized in only a progressive way. When starting on the spiritual path, second-ray people are aware that the manifest world is an organized creation that springs from the heart of God ("The heart revolves"). They are also aware that this creation has an intricate design, with multiple interior organisms that produce an aggregate of living forms, but they know nothing except the general nature of the world. Later on the path, they come to see and grasp the similarity and unity existing between the macrocosm, which is the organism through which the heart of God is working, and the microcosm, which is the organism through which the human soul is working ("two hearts revolve as one"). In other words, they grasp the principle, "As above, so below."

During a more advanced stage, second-ray people are able to comprehend the intricate beauty of the inner relationships existing within the divine Whole, the focal points of energy that act as power and light stations within that Whole, and the circulation of energy between these focal points. One such focal point is the heart center of the solar Logos, which is symbolized by a twelve-petalled lotus. It is the inner point of life within each manifested form ("the twelve within the vehicle"). Another focal point is the heart center of the planetary Logos, which is also symbolized by a twelve-petalled lotus. According to Bailey, the planetary Logos is the heart center

---

[14] A. A. Bailey, *Letters on Occult Meditation* (1922; reprint; New York: Lucis Publishing, Company, 1974), pp. 285, 286; A. A. Bailey, *The Externalisation of the Hierarchy* (1957; reprint; New York: Lucis Publishing Company, 1976), p. 635.

of Shamballa, and the latter is the head or crown center of the planetary life. Thus, the heart center of the planetary Logos carries the energy that inwardly impels and directs the planetary head center ("the twelve within the head"). A third focal point is the human soul, and it is symbolized by a twelve-petalled lotus, the egoic lotus, which is located on the abstract levels of the mental plane ("and the twelve upon the plane of soul endeavor"). These focal points of energy cooperate and work together as a unity ("cooperate as one"). When evoked by a human being, spiritual love emanates from the great heart of love of the solar Logos, passes through the heart center of the planetary Logos, and then reaches the soul.[15]

In the progressive manner outlined above, second-ray people gradually enter into a detailed and integrated comprehension of the divine Whole. While entering into this comprehension, they are urged by their souls to serve others by revealing to them the essential oneness of the many lives ("and thus the work is done").

6. *Wisdom:* After receiving spiritual love on the level of the egoic lotus, second-ray counselors transform it into compassion and positive regard. These two energies illustrate the previously described capacity of inclusive reason ("Two energies achieve this consummation"), because they provide the ability to sense both the greater whole of humanity and the essential worth of each human being. As a result, the counselors become magnetic, attracting those who need assistance. By bringing these two energies down to the level of their etheric chakras, the counselors are able to render service to others. Bailey defines *wisdom* as "love expressing itself in service." As shown in Table 1 (on page 16), the number of petals in either the heart, crown, or brow chakra is a multiple of twelve. Wisdom occurs when the three chakras whose number is a multiple of twelve respond to the energies transmitted from the

[15] Bailey, *Esoteric Psychology*, vol. 2, pp. 393-396; Bailey, *Esoteric Astrology*, p. 47; Bailey, *Discipleship in the New Age*, vol. 1, p. 768.

egoic lotus ("and the three whose number is a twelve respond to the greater twelve"). The heart chakra responds by radiating compassion from itself and controlling the radiation of positive regard from the solar plexus chakra; the crown chakra responds by revealing the nature of someone's problem with perfect clarity; and the brow chakra responds by producing the appropriate words of salvation.[16]

Note that the description for the first five qualities gives the details of the counseling process, whereas the description for the sixth quality shows how the details fit together as a single whole. This organization provides another illustration of inclusive reason, which is the second-ray ability of grasping both the details and the whole.

When centered in the personality, people travel on what could be called the path of knowledge. But when centered in the soul, they travel on the path of understanding. Recipients of the counseling described above are helped in moving from the first path to the second. Because they have been deeply understood, they can understand themselves ("The life is known"). Because they have had a profound experience of love's power, they can prolong the periods in which they express that power in their own lives ("and the years prolonged").

Ray Three

The healer stands and weaves. He gathers from the three, the five, the seven that which is needed for the heart of life. He brings the energies together and makes them serve the third; he thus creates a vortex into which the one distressed must descend and with him goes the healer. And yet they both remain in peace and

---

[16] Bailey, *Letters on Occult Meditation*, p. 286; Bailey, *A Treatise on Cosmic Fire*, pp. 859, 860.

calm. Thus must the angel of the Lord descend into the pool and bring the healing life.[17]

The third section of the preceding chapter described how educators can apply the principles of Maria Montessori and prepare good classroom environments for children. These educators are assumed to be in the position where they can recognize good educational principles formulated by someone else but are unable to discover such principles for themselves. The present section considers third-ray educators who are in a more advanced position. By using their characteristic qualities, they formulate new educational principles and then prepare effective learning environments for various types of people.

1. *Mental illumination:* Advanced third-ray educators are able to have their minds illumined by the mind of God. Through mental discipline, each one temporarily raises the center of consciousness from the mental body to the soul ("The healer stands"). Next, the soul receives intuitive ideas from the mind of God, formulates or weaves abstract principles that embody the ideas, and conveys those principles to the waiting mental body ("and weaves"). This cycle of soul activity ends when the center of consciousness slips back to the mental body.

2. *Power to manifest:* By using the third, fifth, and seventh subrays of their soul ray, third-ray educators manifest the new learning environments that are needed for unfolding the spiritual nature of human beings ("He gathers from the three, the five, the seven that which is needed for the heart of life"). They use the third subray to convert their abstract principles into concrete plans, the fifth subray to maintain the proper emotional feelings, and the seventh subray to direct activities on the physical plane. The learning environments might include addiction treatment facilities, other mental health care facilities, primary and secondary education, holistic living commu-

---

[17] Bailey, *Esoteric Healing,* p. 708.

nities, and schools of philosophy, psychology, and religion. Each environment shows that it has a divine origin by helping its participants to unfold their inner divinity.

3. *Scientific investigation:* The divine plan is an expression of the active intelligence or third-ray quality of God, and it exists on the level of intuitive ideas.[18] After receiving the aspects of the divine plan to which they have been assigned, the educators take them down in three main steps: formulation of abstract principles, construction of mental plans, and then manifestation of those plans in tangible forms. To ensure that the manifested forms are a true downward reflection of the divine plan, they trace the transformation of the energy backward in the upward direction. In other words, they investigate the outer forms, discover the inner patterns that they serve, and then make whatever adjustments are needed so that the forms do in fact serve the divine plan ("He brings the energies together and makes them serve the third"). This is scientific investigation in that the educators begin by studying the outer structures and then infer the relationships and principles that lie behind.

4. *Power to evolve:* Through the foregoing efforts, the educators create learning environments into which distressed people enter and thereby grow in self-mastery ("he thus creates a vortex into which the one distressed must descend"). The evolution of the participants occurs when they learn to evoke their own inner nature, which is the inner divine healer ("and with him goes the healer"), and it occurs in several stages. At the beginning, the participants learn how to be integrated personalities. Later they express the wisdom of the soul and still later the life of the spirit.

5. *Balance:* To express one's inner spiritual qualities, one must follow the middle path between the pairs of opposites. In other words, one must avoid extreme behavior and find the proper balance between rest and activity, inspiration and per-

---

[18] Bailey, *Telepathy and the Etheric Vehicle,* p. 46.

spiration, austerity and indulgence, individual and group activity, meditation and service, and so forth. Advanced educators are able to follow the middle path when manifesting their learning environments, and they design their environments so that each participant is encouraged to follow the middle path ("And yet they both remain in peace and calm").[19]

6. *Power to produce synthesis on the physical plane.* The last sentence of Bailey's symbolic statement has a double meaning. First, through the application of the foregoing qualities, the divine plan manifests in the physical world as new learning environments and brings the experiences needed for the collective evolution of humanity ("Thus must the angel of the Lord descend into the pool and bring the healing life"). Second, because the participants in the environments are encouraged to follow the middle path, the divine qualities of each participant are evoked into his or her physical experience and bring the illumination needed for individual evolution. In this way, third-ray educators have the power to produce synthesis on the physical plane, revealing the oneness of the physical form and divine plan, of the collective and individual, and of the human life and spiritual life.

Ray Four

The healer knows the place where dissonance is found. He also knows the power of sound and the sound which must be heard. Knowing the note to which the fourth great group reacts and linking it to the great Creative Nine, he sounds the note which brings release, the note which will bring absorption into one. He educates the listening ear of him who must be healed; he likewise trains the listening ear of him who must go forth. He knows the manner of the sound which

---

[19] Bailey, *Esoteric Psychology*, vol. 2, pp. 160-163.

brings the healing touch; and also that which says: Depart. And thus the work is done.[20]

Because the fourth-ray formula refers to the egoic lotus, let us consider that concept in more detail. Although the egoic lotus is a concrete symbol, it depicts the nature and characteristics of the soul, which belongs to the abstract levels of the mental plane. The egoic lotus has twelve petals, and each one represents a particular power of the soul. Nine outer petals extend from a common center and cover three central petals. These twelve petals have the appearance of an unopened bud for an undeveloped person, but through evolution they become organized, vitalized, and then opened. Consequently, the egoic lotus provides a dynamic image of how the various powers of the soul unfold over time.

In this book, we are concerned with the meaning of only the nine outer petals. As shown in Table 6 (on page 90), the unfoldment of each outer petal marks a definite stage of evolution, and it occurs when the person has learned the corresponding lesson from his or her experiences. The nine outer petals form three concentric circles, with three petals in each circle. The petals in the largest circle are called the *knowledge* petals, and they embody the wisdom, or abstracted essence of knowledge, needed for intelligent activity on the physical plane. The petals in the middle circle are called the *love* petals, and they embody the wisdom needed for transforming self-centered feelings into inclusive love. The petals in the smallest circle are called the *sacrifice* petals, and they embody the wisdom needed to sacrifice materialistic goals and serve humanity. The knowledge petals unfold first, followed by the love petals, and then by the sacrifice petals.

After bringing harmony to their inner nature, fourth-ray individuals can help other people to overcome inner conflicts and achieve harmony within themselves. Because this helping process is equivalent to performing psychotherapy, we

---

[20] Bailey, *Esoteric Healing*, p. 709.

Table 6. The Nine Outer Petals of the Egoic Lotus.*

First Group of Petals—Knowledge Petals

1. "The *Petal of Knowledge* for the physical plane. Through the breaking of the Law and the ensuing suffering the price of ignorance is paid and knowledge is achieved. This unfoldment is brought about through physical plane experience."

2. "The *Petal of Love* for the physical plane. Unfolds through physical relationships, and the gradual growth of love from love of self to love of others."

3. "The *Petal of Sacrifice* for the physical plane. This unfoldment is brought about through the driving force of circumstances, and not of free will. It is the offering up of the physical body upon the altar of desire—low desire to begin with, but aspiration towards the end, though still desire."

Second Group of Petals—Love Petals

4. "The *Petal of Knowledge,* for the astral plane; unfoldment is brought about by the conscious balancing of the pairs of opposites, and the gradual utilisation of the Law of Attraction and Repulsion."

5. "The *Petal of Love* for the astral plane; unfoldment is brought about through the process of gradually transmuting the love of the subjective nature or of the Self within."

6. "The *Petal of Sacrifice* for the astral plane; unfoldment is brought about by the attitude of man as he consciously endeavors to give up his own desires for the sake of his group. His motive is still somewhat a blind one, and still coloured by the desire for a return of that which he gives and for love from those he seeks to serve, but it is of a much higher order than the blind sacrifice to which a man is driven by circumstances as is the case in the earlier unfoldment."

Table 6. The Nine Outer Petals of the Egoic Lotus (continued).*

Third Group of Petals—Sacrifice Petals
7. "The *Petal of Knowledge* for the mental plane; its unfoldment marks the period wherein the man consciously utilizes all that he has gained or is gaining under the law for the definite benefit of humanity."
8. "The *Petal of Love* on the mental plane is unfolded through the conscious steady application of all the powers of the soul to the service of humanity with no thought of return nor any desire for reward for the immense sacrifice involved."
9. "The *Petal of Sacrifice* for the mental plane: demonstrates as the predominate bias of the soul as seen in a series of many lives spent by the initiate prior to his final emancipation. He becomes in his sphere the 'Great Sacrifice.'"

*Source: A. A. Bailey, *A Treatise on Cosmic Fire* (1925; reprint; New York: Lucis Publishing Company, 1977), pp. 539-542.

shall refer to the healer as the therapist and the recipient as the patient. The explanations for the first three qualities are general in nature and are meant to apply to all patients seeking assistance. The explanations for the last three qualities are more specific, with each one applying to only a subset of patients.

1. *Power to penetrate the depths of matter.* Human evolution proceeds as a series of integrations. A person's first step is integrating the physical body with the emotional body. Subsequent steps include integrating these two with the mental body, integrating these three with the personality as a whole, and integrating the coordinated personality with the soul. Before achieving any of these integrations, a person experiences a period of distress due to sensing the cleavage between the lower integrated parts and the higher part that is next to be integrated. This distress may appear as unrest, frustration, futility, or a

nervous breakdown. If the distress is sufficiently severe, then he or she may seek the understanding help of a competent therapist.

When approached by patients who are suffering from inner discomfort and frustration, experienced fourth-ray therapists have the power to penetrate behind the symptoms of distress and discern the point of cleavage that each patient is encountering. In other words, they are able to recognize the place in the patient's inner constitution where the previously integrated parts are in conflict with the higher part that is seeking integration ("The healer knows the place where dissonance is found").

2. *Harmony of the spheres:* Experienced therapists are able to perceive the underlying harmony that already exists between the various spheres or parts of each patient's inner constitution. For instance, they know that the power to produce the needed integration and to end the sensed duality lies within the patient—because the next part to be integrated is essentially more powerful than the lower waiting ones ("He also knows the power of sound"). The patient's discomfort, pain, and distress are actually symptoms of aspiration and are the reactions of the integrated parts to the higher part that is seeking integration. The lower waiting parts are negative and receptive, whereas the higher part is positive and dynamic. They also know that the psychological crisis must be faced and understood by the patient ("and the sound which must be heard") before he or she can make any further progress. The human race has progressed to its present point in evolution through facing such difficulties, and each person progresses in the same way. Because this crisis is an integral part of the evolutionary process, its occurrence actually indicates progress and opportunity rather than disaster and failure. The psychological crisis brings the need for strenuous effort, and it will eventually bring a sense of gain and freedom when surmounted and solved. After achieving this integration, however, the patient

must eventually repeat the same cycle on a higher level by facing another inner conflict.[21]

3. *Synthesis of true beauty:* Figure 1 (on page 3) shows that the human constitution consists of four main groups: monad, spiritual triad, soul, and personality. Bailey's formula refers to the personality as the "fourth great group" because it is the fourth or lowest of these groups. The experienced therapist knows the particular words to which the patient's personality responds and that link it with the nine outer petals of the egoic lotus ("Knowing the note to which the fourth great group reacts and linking it to the great Creative Nine"). In other words, the therapist can speak in a way that conveys new understanding, the latter being symbolized as new activity or unfoldment within the petals of the egoic lotus. Due to this ability, the therapist provides effective instruction on how to release the power of the higher part that is seeking integration ("he sounds the note which brings release"). After the power of the higher part is released, it brings the lower parts of the patient's inner constitution into a synthesis of true harmony and unity ("the note which brings absorption into one").

4. *Dual aspects of desire:* Selfish desire is a definite hindrance for some people but an asset for others. Because fourth-ray therapists understand these two aspects of desire, their method of working with desire depends on the needs of each patient. First, suppose that a particular patient is experiencing an inner conflict between personality and soul, which is the same type of conflict considered in the second section of chapter 2. This conflict arises when the patient senses the qualities of his or her soul ray and contrasts those qualities with the self-centered activities of daily life. Here, the therapist educates the patient on how to heal or overcome the desire of the personality, which must be done before the personality can be an instrument of the soul ("He educates the listening ear of him who must be

---

[21] Bailey, *Esoteric Psychology,* vol. 2, pp. 427, 428.

healed"). The necessary approach includes observing the personality in an objective way, evoking the wisdom of the soul, and then transmuting self-centered motives into unselfish ones.

On the other hand, suppose that the patient is experiencing the cleavage between the elements of the personality and the personality as a whole. This cleavage becomes evident when the patient wishes to fulfill a desire to achieve influence and power in some field of endeavor but is prevented from doing so by a lack of coordination. For instance, there might be an inability to concentrate, breaks in the continuity of interests, unfinished tasks, and frustration. Now, the therapist provides training on how to go forth and fulfill desire, which the patient must do as the next step in his or her evolution ("he likewise trains the listening ear of him who must go forth"). For instance, the patient might be assisted in having the right diet and physical exercise; eliminating the sense of guilt along with such concomitants as revolt, suspicion, and an inferiority complex; having the right interests, education, and vocational training; and developing any creative faculty that would satisfy the desire to be noticed and to contribute.

5. *Power to express divinity*: Next, consider people who are facing the cleavage between their physical and emotional bodies. Such people are centered in their physical bodies, which means that they are concerned primarily with experiencing physical pleasures without any intelligent understanding of the environment. But they also dimly sense the presence of feelings and an innate conscience, the latter being an intuitive urge to higher living. This particular cleavage is generally integrated by children as part of their natural development, but it can also occur in adults, producing many of the problem cases found in psychiatric clinics. In either case, the experienced therapist knows the method of treatment that brings the patient's creative imagination and power of choice into activity, which will then heal the cleavage ("He knows the manner of sound which brings the healing touch"). According to Bailey, these two factors "are the signal evidence of divinity in man." The creative imagination engenders the sense of fantasy and per-

ception of beauty. Making choices helps to unfold the innate conscience and involves such considerations as why, wherefore, and to what end. The emotional nature is provided with constructive outlets only when the creative imagination is balanced and motivated by right choices and higher values.[22]

6. *Power to reveal the path*: And finally, consider patients facing the cleavage between their emotional and mental bodies. They are aware of strong and compelling desires, which keep them dwelling in the realm of longing, hoping, and wishing. But their thoughts bring the conviction that they are unable to satisfy their desires and doubts about whether their goals are even worthwhile. Due to this cleavage, they may feel frustrated and depressed, become inactive, escape through various fantasies, and even consider suicide. Or they may be compulsively driven to fulfill their desires, which may break them either physically or psychologically. When working with such a person, the experienced therapist knows the method of treatment that develops the patient's own mental power of discrimination, which then reveals the proper path on which to move ("and also that which says: Depart"). Through effective use of the intellect, the patient differentiates between essentials and nonessentials, between right direction and wrong goals, and between practical programs and activities doomed to failure ("And thus the work is done").[23]

Ray Five

That which has been given must be used; that which emerges from within the given mode will find its place within the healer's plan. That which is hidden must be seen and from the three, great knowledge

---

[22] Bailey, *Glamour: A World Problem*, pp. 108, 109; Bailey, *Esoteric Psychology*, vol. 2, pp. 428, 429.
[23] Bailey, *Esoteric Psychology*, vol. 2, pp. 421, 422.

will emerge. For these the healer seeks. To these the
healer adds the two which are as one, and so the fifth
must play its part and the five must play its part and
the five must function as if one. The energies descend,
pass through and disappear, leaving the one who
could respond with karma yet to dissipate and taking with them him who may not thus respond and
so must likewise disappear.[24]

After fifth-ray people attain the second initiation, they are
excellent researchers and can serve others by achieving the
advanced stages of raja yoga. The problems that they investigate could be from any department of human knowledge
such as religion, science, or economics. Their characteristic
qualities are described next.

1. *Emergence into form and out of form:* The mental plane
consists of seven subplanes that fall into two groups: the lowest four subplanes are the concrete or form levels; the top three
subplanes are the abstract or formless levels. The first quality
refers to two different types of emergence: the emergence of
an abstract intuition within the mental body on the concrete
levels; and the emergence of consciousness within the soul on
the abstract levels.

Fifth-ray researchers are able to experience these two
types of emergence by mastering the first three stages of raja
yoga. The first stage of raja yoga is called *concentration.* In the
research context, concentration involves choosing a seed
thought concerned with some world problem and giving oneself a mental circular boundary, sometimes called a ring-pass-
not, that allows only thoughts about the significance, meaning,
and implications of the seed thought. This circular boundary
must then be used to confine one's thinking ("That which has
been given must be used"). Whenever thoughts stray outside
the boundary, they are replaced with the seed thought.

The second stage of raja yoga is called *meditation.* Each
researcher enters this stage when he or she begins to sense the

---

[24] Bailey, *Esoteric Healing,* p. 710.

abstract truth or inner relationships being veiled by the seed thought. Initially there may be difficulty in grasping and touching the truth. But with the struggle to comprehend, little by little the abstract truth emerges from within the circular boundary on the concrete levels of the mental plane and finds its place within the researcher's thinking and planning ("that which emerges from within the given mode will find its place within the healer's plan").

The second phrase of Bailey's formula has a double meaning, because it also describes the third stage of raja yoga, called *contemplation*. At the beginning of this stage, the center of the researcher's consciousness moves out of the mental body on the concrete levels of the mental plane and emerges from within the soul on the abstract levels, enabling the soul to play an active role within the inquiry ("that which emerges from within the given mode will find its place within the healer's plan"). Meanwhile, the mental body is quiescent and is oriented to receiving abstract thoughts from the soul.[25]

2. *Power to make the Voice of the Silence heard*: The soul is the storehouse for wisdom, which is the abstracted essence learned from experience, and the soul is also the instrument for expressing principles or abstract thoughts. When abstract thinking is a response of memory rather than the product of a direct realization, it is limited and can produce illusions. During the contemplation stage, the soul can avoid those illusions because it has the power to evoke insights from an even deeper part of the inner self, which is the spiritual mind. These insights are direct perceptions of truth, and they are sometimes called "the Voice of the Silence." Through this evocation or higher alignment, what previously has been hidden is clearly seen ("That which is hidden must be seen"). After receiving the insights, the soul uses them to guide its expression of abstract thoughts.[26]

3. *Manifestation of the great white light*: When the center of the researcher's consciousness shifts back into the mental

---

[25] A. A. Bailey, *From Intellect to Intuition* (1932; reprint; New York: Lucis Publishing Company, 1974), pp. 113, 132-144.
[26] Bailey, *A Treatise on White Magic*, pp. 515, 516.

body, the contemplation stage ends and the fourth stage of raja yoga, called *illumination*, begins. The mental body becomes active and formulates concrete knowledge that embodies both the wisdom from the soul and the insights from the spiritual mind. From this triple blending of the lights of knowledge, wisdom, and insight, great understanding will emerge regarding the original seed thought ("and from the three, great knowledge will emerge"). For instance, the researcher might have new ideas that bear witness to the divine plan, new discoveries regarding human beings and nature, or new inventions that can improve human circumstances.

4. *Revelation of the way*: The fifth stage of raja yoga is called *inspiration*, and it is described in the remainder of Bailey's formula. After developing a deep understanding regarding a particular issue, the researcher senses a longing or desire to see this understanding brought to earth and improve some world condition. However, the implementation of any spiritual vision is never the work of one person. Only when the vision has been sensed by the many can it appear in physical form. Thus, for the purpose of materializing the new understanding, the researcher seeks the best way of communicating it with others and attracting their help in return ("For these the healer seeks"). The basic strategy is to touch a large number of people with a brief capsule of the new ideas, which then will attract those special individuals who are sufficiently ready, able, and interested to hear more. After examining the various approaches that are available for publicity, the researcher discerns and chooses, dissects and analyzes, until the best plan is revealed.[27]

5. *Initiating activity*: The next step is to initiate the activities of the plan for publicity. Here, the researcher adds the energies of the etheric body and dense physical body, the two parts of the physical vehicle ("To these the healer adds the two which are as one"). If the plan is successfully implemented, then

---

[27] Bailey, *A Treatise on White Magic*, p. 368.

the lights of knowledge, wisdom, and insight, which are the lights of the fifth or mental plane, will play their part in the evolution of human consciousness ("and so the fifth must play its part"). For the plan to be successfully implemented, the lower five parts of the human constitution must make a contribution ("and the five must play its part"). The wisdom of the soul must guide the mind, the mind must preserve the details of the plan and control the lower nature, the emotional body must preserve the desire to implement the plan and provide the capacity to cooperate with others, the etheric body must give the power to act and be energetic, and the dense physical body must manipulate and function within the tangible world.

The researcher might have the tendency to promote the plan for publicity in an unbalanced manner. For instance, one might be obsessed with one's own ideas on the mental level, be a fanatic on the emotional level, or exhaust oneself on the physical level. To avoid the various possibilities of undue emphasis, the lower five parts of the constitution must function and work together in an integrated and harmonious way ("and the five must function as if one").[28]

6. *Purification with fire.* At this point, the researcher has publicized the new ideas and attracted various listeners who wish to study them in detail. So that the new ideas can do their work, the researcher transforms them into new theories, demonstrations, experiments, mechanical devices, or audio-visual presentations, which are then communicated to and understood by the listeners ("The energies descend, pass through and disappear"). Fire is the symbol of the intellect.[29] Through the explanations, the fiery force of the new ideas purifies the thinking of each listener—leaving any belief or attitude that is still consistent with the new ideas and taking away any belief or attitude that is not consistent and so has been understood

[28] Bailey, *Esoteric Psychology,* vol. 2, pp. 369, 370.
[29] Bailey, *A Treatise on White Magic,* p. 250.

as being false ("leaving the one who could respond with karma yet to dissipate and taking with them him who may not thus respond and so must likewise disappear").

The foregoing six qualities encompass all five stages of raja yoga. Bailey summarizes these stages in the following way:

1) *Concentration.* This is the act of concentrating the mind, learning to focus it and so use it.

2) *Meditation.* The prolonged focussing of the attention in any direction and the steady holding of the mind on any desired idea.

3) *Contemplation.* An activity of the soul, detached from the mind, which is held in a state of quiescence.

4) *Illumination.* This is the result of the three preceding processes, and involves the carrying down into the brain consciousness of the knowledge achieved.

5) *Inspiration.* The result of illumination, as it demonstrates in the life of service.[30]

The mastery of each stage leads sequentially to the next one; they lift a person out of the realm of feeling into the realm of knowledge and then into the realm of intuitive illumination.

Ray Six

Cleaving the waters, let the power descend, the healer cries. He minds not how the waters may respond; they oft bring stormy waves and dire and dreadful hap-

---

[30] Bailey, *From Intellect to Intuition*, p. 99.

penings. The end is good. The trouble will be ended
when the storm subsides and energy has fulfilled its
charted destiny. Straight to the heart the power is forced
to penetrate, and into every channel, nadi, nerve
and spleen the power must seek a passage and a way
and thus confront the enemy who has effected
entrance and settled down to live. Ejection—ruthless,
sudden and complete—is undertaken by the one
who sees naught else but perfect functioning and brooks
no interference. This perfect functioning opens thus
the door to life eternal or to life on earth for yet a
little while.[31]

The four traditional elements of alchemy are earth, water,
fire, and air. These elements are sometimes used to characterize
and symbolize the four lowest planes: earth for the physical world,
water for the emotional nature, fire for the mind, and air for
the buddhic plane.[32] Just as the fifth-ray method of service was
primarily concerned with the fiery force of the mind, the
sixth-ray method is primarily concerned with the watery reactions of the emotional nature.

Emotional reactions in the form of glamours can spoil any
service being rendered. For instance, common glamours are
the feeling that there is no way but one's own way, the feeling
of being superior to those being served, and the feeling of self-
righteousness due to rendering service. When individuals
have the sixth ray as their soul ray and are devoted to truth,
they can overcome their glamours and serve the divine plan,
a process that we describe next.

1. *Overcoming the waters of the emotional nature.* Before
engaging in some form of service, advanced sixth-ray servers
pause and analyze their feelings, which are the waters of the
emotional nature, and discover whether any glamours are

[31] Bailey, *Esoteric Healing*, p. 711.
[32] Bailey, *A Treatise on White Magic*, pp. 248-250.

present ("Cleaving the waters"). So that their service is truly helpful to others, they endeavor to overcome any glamours that they recognize. Their approach is to focus their consciousness onto the mental plane, gather the lights of the mind and of the soul, and then pour those blended lights down upon the identified glamours ("let the power descend"). Being focussed on the mental plane is equivalent to being detached and objective toward the glamours. When the servers face and accept the truths that are revealed to them ("the healer cries"), their glamours disappear.[33]

2. *Endurance and fearlessness.* The dissipation of a glamour requires that the mind be used as the bridge between the light of the soul and the dark places of the emotional nature. This bridging relationship is unpleasant and possibly terrifying, because one must confront the actual truth about oneself. By using the qualities of endurance and fearlessness, the servers can observe their emotional reactions in a calm and dispassionate way without self-justification, resistance, or resentment ("He minds not how the waters may respond"). Such observation often brings awareness of pride and vanity, self-deception, and mistakes ("they oft bring stormy waves and dire and dreadful happenings"). By persevering to the end, they find that the actual elimination of a glamour is a satisfying experience ("The end is good").[34]

3. *Power to kill out desire.* The various stages of raja yoga were defined as part of the commentary for the fifth-ray formula. The power to eradicate a given glamour, which is a form of selfish desire, is obtained by accomplishing the first two stages of raja yoga. The first stage, concentration, consists of holding the attention on the glamour. The second stage, meditation, consists of using analysis, discrimination, and right thought to

---

[33] Bailey, *Esoteric Psychology,* vol. 2, pp. 136, 137; Bailey, *Glamour: A World Problem,* pp. 204, 210.

[34] Bailey, *Glamour: A World Problem,* pp. 145, 204.

deal with the glamour, while at the same time being guided by intuitions from the soul. The glamour will be ended when all distractions subside during the concentration stage and when the illumined mind has achieved the necessary realizations during the meditation stage ("The trouble will be ended when the storm subsides and energy has fulfilled its charted destiny").

4. *Self-immolation*: The emotional body is an organic machine that reacts to outer conditions according to its inner programming, and the latter is a pattern of beliefs held in the mind. For a given glamour to disappear, the light of the mind must be forced by the light of the soul to penetrate straight to the associated inner programming, which is the essence, real meaning, or heart of the glamour ("Straight to the heart the power is forced to penetrate"). In particular, one must seek out every concept, attitude, opinion, and self-statement that creates, energizes, conditions, and preserves the glamour ("and into every channel, nadi, nerve and spleen the power must seek a passage and way"). The next step is to confront those beliefs—which means to inquire about their truth or falsehood—because they have power only as long as they are accepted and allowed to live inside one's consciousness ("and thus confront the enemy who has effected entrance and settled down to live"). This confrontation results in the sacrifice or immolation of a false part of the self.

5. *Spurning that which is not desired*: Through the application of the earlier steps, sixth-ray servers achieve the realization that any given glamour is caused by an identification with the objects of desire, with the personality, and with what is material. Spurning of this identification—in an abrupt, sudden, and complete way—is undertaken when the servers recognize the fact that they are the Self and nothing else, that they are perfect spiritual reality and not any mental illusion that would interfere with the expression of their reality ("Ejection—ruthless, sudden and complete—is undertaken by the one who sees naught else but perfect functioning and brooks no interfer-

ence"). By spurning the underlying cause of the glamour, they are able to dispel the glamour itself.[35]

6. *Power to detach oneself.* Through the recognition of their spiritual identity, advanced servers gain the power to detach themselves from the material world and enter the eternal world of the soul ("This perfect functioning opens thus the door to life eternal"). Entering the soul's world is equivalent to achieving the contemplation stage of raja yoga. During this stage, the soul reveals to the poised and peaceful mind the next step to be taken in the divine plan for humanity, which is received as an intuitive understanding of human needs and how to meet those needs. Because these servers can avoid glamour, the downflow of that understanding floods their emotional nature with effective unselfish love, devotion to the divine plan, and the desire to serve that plan. As a result, they return to the material world and help meet the needs of their fellow human beings ("or to life on earth").[36] Because this entering and returning is a cyclic process, each of its phases lasts for only a brief amount of time ("for yet a little while") and then the cycle is repeated. As expressed in Bailey's Esoteric Catechism, "I look above, I help below."[37]

Ray Seven

Energy and force must meet each other and thus the work is done. Colour and sound in ordered sequence must meet and blend and thus the work of magic can proceed. Substance and spirit must evoke each other and, passing through the centre of the one who

---

[35] A. A. Bailey, *The Rays and the Initiations* (1960; reprint; New York: Lucis Publishing Company, 1976), p. 5; Bailey, *Glamour: A World Problem*, pp. 242, 243, 263.

[36] Bailey, *Esoteric Psychology,* vol. 2, pp. 135-137.

[37] A. A. Bailey, *Initiation, Human and Solar* (1922; reprint; New York: Lucis Publishing Company, 1974), p. 213.

seeks to aid, produce the new and good. The healer energises thus with life the failing life, driving it forth or anchoring it yet more deeply in the place of destiny. All seven must be used and through the seven there must pass the energies the need requires, creating the new man who has for ever been and will for ever be, and either here or there.[38]

Magic occurs whenever mental images are translated into physical reality. Any activity of magic falls into one of two categories. If the activity is guided by the illumination of the soul, it is called *white magic*; but if its purpose is to fulfill self-centered ambition, it is called *black magic*. Building a physical organization according to a mental pattern is an activity of magic because it creates an outer appearance of that pattern. As discussed earlier, first-ray people have the peculiar mission of destroying outmoded organizations. In contrast, by using their characteristic qualities, seventh-ray people can apply the principles of white magic and build new organizations on the physical plane.

1. *Power to create:* To create an efficient organization, one must build the outer form so that it is the material representation of a well-formulated mental plan. In other words, one must unite material energy with mental force ("Energy and force must meet each other"). After seventh-ray people master the concentration stage of raja yoga, they can unite matter and mind, and thus they have the power to create efficient organizations ("and thus the work is done"). For instance, they might be executives who reorganize existing political, religious, or educational institutions along newer lines, managers who eliminate factors that prevent their corporations from being efficient, or organizers of new movements that embody new ideals.

2. *Power to think:* Mastering the meditation stage of raja yoga enables one to unite a higher pair of opposites—the

---

[38] Bailey, *Esoteric Healing,* p. 712.

mind and soul. The approach is to be focussed in the mental body and oriented to receiving abstract thoughts from the soul. Then, by using the power to think, one must create an ordered mental plan that embodies the abstract thoughts ("Colour and sound in ordered sequence must meet and blend"). Afterwards, one can proceed with the magical work of manifesting that plan on the physical plane ("and thus the work of magic can proceed").

3. *Mental power.* Mastering the contemplation stage of raja yoga gives one the mental power to unite an even higher pair of opposites—the soul and mind of God. Although residing on the abstract levels of the mental plane, the soul is substantial in the sense that it has a definite form that evolves over time, and this evolution is symbolized by the unfoldment of the nine petals listed in Table 6 (on page 90). On the other hand, the mind of God is spiritual in the sense that it exists in a higher or more subtle dimension. Thus, Bailey's formula refers to this highest pair of opposites as "substance and spirit." The approach here is to shift the center of one's consciousness into the soul. For one to be a conscious exponent of the divine plan, two evocations must then occur: the soul must evoke from the mind of God an intuitive understanding of the immediate aspect of the divine plan and of one's own part in that evolutionary process; and the mind of God must evoke from the soul an appreciation of and devotion for the divine plan ("Substance and spirit must evoke each other"). These evoked responses pass through the mind where they are transformed into a new and better mental plan ("and, passing through the centre of the one who seeks to aid, produce the new and good").

4. *Power to vivify.* As indicated by the three previous qualities, advanced organizers can unite three different pairs of opposites: matter and mind, mind and soul, and soul and mind of God. Through bringing all three pairs into relationship, they can perform white magic and manifest ideals that embody as much of the divine plan as humanity can currently produce in form upon the earth. As a result, they have the power to viv-

ify a dying organization, community, or nation that has fallen into crystallized, sectarian, or materialistic attitudes ("The healer energises thus with life the failing life"). By bringing in new ideals, they drive out obsolete methods or increase the potency and effectiveness of those methods that have not yet fulfilled their true destiny ("driving it forth or anchoring it yet more deeply in the place of destiny").

5. *Power to cooperate.* Seventh-ray organizers have the power to choose carefully their co-workers and to cooperate with them. For an organization to be successful, representatives from all seven rays must be included, and these seven types must have sufficient autonomy to bring through the energies that the need requires ("All seven must be used and through the seven there must pass the energies the need requires"). For instance, first-ray workers can make a powerful impact on the minds of their listeners by emphasizing important governing principles. Second-ray workers can gather students and teach them new ideas. Third-ray workers can stimulate the intellect of humanity by writing books and articles. Fourth-ray workers can harmonize new ideas with older ones so that there is no dangerous break. Fifth-ray workers can work with hypotheses, proving them either true or false. Sixth-ray workers can teach people to recognize the truth and to desire those ideals whose time has come to be manifested on earth. Meanwhile, seventh-ray organizers help by synthesizing the activities of their co-workers. They ensure that the unified effort embodies their assigned portion of the divine plan and invites the participation of humanity.[39]

6. *Revelation of the beauty of God:* By applying the preceding qualities, a seventh-ray organizer builds a physical movement, society, or association that provides a revelation of the plan of God. After receiving this revelation, humanity will manifest more of its spiritual nature, which has always existed and will always exist, in any one of several fields of work ("cre-

---

[39] Bailey, *Esoteric Psychology,* vol. 2, pp. 140-145.

ating the new man who has for ever been and will for ever be, and either here or there"). For instance in the religious field, people will understand the inner significance of their own faiths and the essential unity of all faiths. In the political field, they will develop an international consciousness and will gradually establish a brotherhood of nations based on mutual need, mutual understanding, and mutual helpfulness. And in the scientific field, they will unfold their latent powers and learn more about the hidden wonders of the universe.[40]

---

[40] Bailey, *The Externalisation of the Hierarchy*, p. 670; Bailey, *Esoteric Psychology*, vol. 1, pp. 172-179.

Chapter 4

---※---

METHODS OF ESOTERIC HEALING

First keep the peace within yourself,
then you can also bring peace to others.
—Thomas à Kempis

The word *esoteric* has several meanings. First, it refers to what is inner and cannot readily be perceived. In the case of a method of esoteric healing, the healing energies are too subtle to be seen or heard by ordinary human faculties. Second, esoteric refers to what is intended for or understood by only an inner group of disciples or initiates. The methods of esoteric healing presented in this chapter also share that characteristic. To accomplish any of the methods, a person must have achieved a certain measure of self-discipline and enlightenment. According to Bailey, "even if the techniques or the seven modes of healing—relating as they do to the energies of the seven rays—were exactly imparted to you, it would be rare indeed to find a healer who was competent to use them in this interim period in world affairs."[1]

The theosophical concept of initiation was introduced in chapter 1, and it is a way of quantifying the progress that a per-

---

[1] A. A. Bailey, *Esoteric Healing* (1953; reprint; New York: Lucis Publishing Company, 1978), p. 693.

son has made on the spiritual path. According to our understanding, the esoteric methods given for the first, second, fifth, and seventh rays assume that the healer has achieved the third initiation, which is well beyond the present attainment of the vast majority of people. Although we may not be able to apply those methods at the present time, we may still profit from considering their theory and their indications of future possibilities. On the other hand, the methods given for the third, fourth, and sixth rays require a lesser attainment and are probably within reach of many readers of this book.

The methods of esoteric healing described in this chapter fall into two basic categories: radiatory healing and pranic healing. The purpose of *radiatory healing* is to transmit various spiritual qualities to a patient, including spiritual purpose, compassion, mental clarity, and inner peace. On the other hand, the purpose of *pranic healing* is to transmit a type of energy called prana, magnetism, or vitality, which replaces or reinforces the vital energy within a patient and brings physical health. As we shall show, the symbolic formulas for rays one, three, four, and six describe techniques of radiatory healing, and the symbolic formulas for rays two, five, and seven describe techniques of pranic healing.

The first three rays are the major rays and the last four rays are the minor ones. As illustrated in figure 1 (on page 3), the monad has three qualities that correspond to the three major rays. When a monadic quality is expressed through the soul, the seven qualities of the soul (described in chapter 2) become the seven subrays of the monadic quality. In the method of esoteric healing given for each major ray, the healer must first become centered in the soul and then evoke the corresponding monadic quality. In the method given for each minor ray, the healer must display the corresponding subray of a monadic quality.

Ray One

Let the dynamic force which rules the hearts of all within Shamballa come to my aid, for I am worthy of that aid. Let it descend unto the third, pass to the fifth and focus on the seventh. These words mean not what doth at sight appear. The third, the fifth, the seventh lie within the first and come from out the Central Sun of spiritual livingness. The highest then awakens within the one who knows and within the one who must be healed and thus the two are one. This is mystery deep. The blending of the healing force effects the work desired; it may bring death, that great release, and re-establish thus the fifth, the third, the first, but not the seventh.[2]

Our planet has both a dense physical body and an etheric or vital body. The planetary dense physical body is the familiar tangible world of sensory perceptions. The planetary etheric body includes the etheric bodies of all forms existing on our planet as integral and intrinsic parts, and it is whole, unbroken, and continuous. Even when the dense physical bodies of any two human beings are separated by many miles, their etheric bodies are still connected by way of the planetary etheric body. The aura consists of the emanations, or the outgoing vibratory effects, of the human etheric body, and it can convey etheric, emotional, mental, and spiritual energies. The human etheric body is substantial in nature, whereas the aura is essentially radiation and extends from that etheric body in all directions. The aura vibrates and propagates within the planetary etheric body, and it enables subtle energies to pass from one human etheric body to another.[3]

In radiatory healing, the healer uses his or her aura for transmitting spiritual qualities to the patient. Both vertical and horizontal alignments are required: vertical alignment between the healer's monad, spiritual triad, soul, and personality; and horizontal alignment between the personalities of the healer

---

[2] Bailey, *Esoteric Healing,* pp. 706, 707.

[3] A. A. Bailey, *Telepathy and the Etheric Vehicle* (1950; reprint; New York: Lucis Publishing Company, 1975), pp. 97-99; Bailey, *Esoteric Healing,* p. 645.

Table 7. Lines of Transmission in Radiatory Healing.

Radiation of Will	Radiation of Love-Wisdom	Radiation of Active Intelligence
Monad: will	Monad: love-wisdom	Monad: active intelligence
Spiritual will	Spiritual love	Spiritual mind
Sacrifice petals of egoic lotus	Love petals of egoic lotus	Knowledge petals of egoic lotus
Etheric body in its higher aspect	Emotional body	Mental body or concrete mind
Crown and brow chakras of healer	Heart and solar plexus chakras of healer	Throat chakra of healer
Crown chakra of patient	Heart and solar plexus chakras of patient	Throat chakra of patient
Aids the patient in becoming aligned with a source of motivation higher than the personality	Aids the patient in experiencing compassion and inner peace	Aids the patient in strengthening and clarifying the mind

and patient. As shown in Table 7, three different lines of transmission are possible. A stream of energy can originate from any of the three qualities of the monad (the healer's essential spiritual nature) and then pass through the spiritual triad (the reflection of that nature in the field of manifestation), through the egoic lotus (where the healer has an abstract understanding of the inner qualities), through the personality (where the inner qualities are expressed), through the healer's etheric chakras (which radiate the qualities via the aura), through the patient's etheric chakras (which receive the emanations), and finally through the patient's personality (which responds to the emanations). The first-ray formula describes one of these lines, namely, the one that extends from the will or first-ray quality of the monad.

According to esoteric philosophy, Shamballa and the monad are closely related. As discussed in chapter 3, Shamballa is the name of the planetary center "where the Will of God is known." In the final stages of initiation, the monad becomes the revealer of the Will of God, which is the purpose of the planetary Logos. The world of Shamballa is similar to the state of being of the monad because it is a world of pure energy, light, and directed force that exists in a dimension beyond the manifest world. Just as a human being has a personality, soul, and monad (or spirit), the planetary life can be thought of as having the same divisions. The fourth or human kingdom of nature is the planetary personality, the fifth or spiritual kingdom of nature is the planetary soul, and Shamballa is the planetary monad. Because the role of Shamballa within the planetary macrocosm is similar to that of the monad within the human microcosm, the word *Shamballa* is sometimes used to refer to the monad. For instance, when the consciousness and life of the monad are fully expressed through a human being, Bailey has remarked, "Shamballa is consummated in him." For these reasons, we shall interpret the word *Shamballa,* which appears in the first sentence of the formula, as referring to the monad.[4]

To understand the rest of the formula, it may be helpful to contrast three different levels of will. The will of the spiritual triad is called the spiritual will or the *will-to-good,* and it applies insights and spiritual perception to serve the divine plan. The will of the soul is called the *goodwill,* and it applies wisdom and group awareness to serve humanity. The transformation of either will into etheric energy is sometimes called *dynamic purpose,* and it is the intention of displaying that will through dynamic activity in the physical world.

Suppose that you wish to implement the process outlined in the first column of Table 7 (on page 112). Your first step is to invoke the monadic will, which rules all other aspects of the monad ("Let the dynamic force which rules the hearts of all within Shamballa come to my aid"). This invocation will be successful only if you have sufficient spiritual development ("for I am worthy of that aid"). In particular, you must merge the personality self-will with the sacrificial will of the soul, creating the soul-infused personality, and then use the soul-infused personality to invoke the monadic will.

When your invocation is successful, the monadic will descends to the third or atmic plane ("Let it descend unto the third") where it is experienced as the will-to-good. Note that this method of esoteric healing does not require that you make direct contact with the monadic will; it is sufficient to make indirect contact by experiencing that quality as the will-to-good. The will-to-good then passes to the soul on the fifth or mental plane ("pass to the fifth") where it is transformed into the goodwill. Afterwards, both the will-to-good and the goodwill

---

[4] A. A. Bailey, *Discipleship in the New Age,* vol. 2 (1955; reprint; New York: Lucis Publishing Company, 1972), pp. 291-293; A. A. Bailey, *The Rays and the Initiations* (1960; reprint; New York: Lucis Publishing Company, 1976), p. 147.

are focussed in the etheric body on the seventh or physical plane where they are transformed into the energy of dynamic purpose ("and focus on the seventh").

Although it may appear that the monadic will is different from the will-to-good, goodwill, and dynamic purpose, this difference is an illusion ("These words mean not what doth at sight appear"). The will-to-good, goodwill, and dynamic purpose are the reflections of the monadic will on the lower levels—which means that these lower types of will are contained latently within the first type and come from out of the monad, which is the essential spiritual center of human life ("The third, the fifth, the seventh lie within the first and come from out the Central Sun of spiritual livingness").

The crown chakra is the highest chakra within the etheric body. After the foregoing alignments are achieved, your crown chakra awakens with dynamic purpose ("The highest then awakens within the one who knows"), and your next step is using your brow chakra to radiate this energy toward the patient. At several places in her writings, Bailey indicates that you must have attained the third initiation to accomplish this step. Perhaps her clearest statement along these lines is the following passage, in which *ajna* is the Sanskrit name for the brow chakra:

> In this third initiation it is the ajna centre (the centre between the eyebrows) which is stimulated. This is a fact of great interest, because it is at this initiation that the disciple begins consciously and creatively to direct the energies being made available to him, doing so via the ajna centre and directed towards humanity as a whole.[5]

After dynamic purpose radiates out from your brow chakra, the crown chakra of the patient awakens with the

---

[5] Bailey, *The Rays and the Initiations,* p. 689.

energy, provided that he or she has the capacity of respond-
ing ("The highest then awakens . . . within the one who must
be healed"). If the capacity is there, then both you and the patient
would be motivated by an incentive higher than that of the personality, resulting in a spirit of cooperation and oneness ("and
thus the two are one"). However, the patient's capacity to reg-
ister the will radiation depends upon the depth of his or her
own spiritual unfoldment ("This is mystery deep"). In Bailey's
words, the patient must be "highly developed."[6] If the necessary unfoldment is lacking, then the patient would simply be
unaffected by the radiation.

The final step is to gain knowledge, both occult and scientific, about the proper application of this type of radiatory
healing to a patient having an illness. Here, an understanding of some additional concepts regarding the inner human
constitution is necessary. A person has two streams of energy
that pass from the soul to the physical body. The *consciousness
stream* enables a person to be rational, self-conscious, and self-
directing. It is anchored or has its seat in the crown chakra,
controls the brain, and operates through the nervous system.
The *life stream* carries the regenerating power and coordinat-
ing energy to the physical organism and keeps the body whole.
It is anchored or focused in the heart chakra, controls the circulation of blood, and animates every atom of the body. These
two energy streams enable a person to be a conscious living
entity, capable of functioning intelligently in the physical
world.[7]

When the will radiation blends with the crown chakra of
the patient, it could have two different effects ("The blending
of the healing force effects the work desired"). First, the radiation may promote recovery by stimulating the crown chakra.
The goal is to attract, if possible, a fuller inflow of the consciousness

---

[6] Bailey, *Esoteric Healing*, p. 551.
[7] A. A. Bailey, *A Treatise on White Magic* (1914; reprint; New York: Lucis Publishing
Company, 1974), pp. 495, 496.

stream to the crown chakra, which would enable the life stream to carry more regenerating power to the heart chakra. As a result, the patient's own "livingness" would bring about the desired cure, primarily through the natural and normal means of adequate vitality. However, the healing process may cause a temporary aggravation in the severity of the patient's symptoms—such as a rise in temperature—which is similar to the experience in homeopathic treatment. You should be prepared for such an eventuality and take the physical steps that would offset any physical reactions that are too severe.[8] Bailey describes the foregoing process in the following way:

> Those healers who have triadal consciousness and can exercise the potency of the monadic life and will, via the Spiritual Triad, will always be successful healers; they will make no mistakes, for they will have accurate spiritual perception; this will give them knowledge as to the possibility of cure, and by the use of the will they can then work safely and with power on the head centre of the patient. They will necessarily confine their healing powers to those who live focussed in the head. They will stimulate the soul, there anchored, into effective activity, thus promoting a true self-healing.[9]

On the other hand, the will radiation may assist the patient in the process of dying ("it may bring death"). Death requires that both the consciousness and life streams be released from the physical body, producing complete loss of consciousness and disintegration of the body ("that great release"). During sleep only the consciousness stream is withdrawn, which means that the person's consciousness or sense of awareness is focused elsewhere. But in death, both streams

---

[8] Bailey, *Esoteric Healing*, pp. 541, 707.

[9] Bailey, *Esoteric Healing*, p. 547.

are withdrawn. According to Bailey, the release or abstraction of these energy streams occurs at one of three possible openings or "orifices of exit": the exit at the top of the head, which is used by people who are spiritually advanced; the exit just below the apex of the heart, which is used by aspirants and people of goodwill; and the exit in the region of the solar plexus, which is used by undeveloped and emotionally polarized people. During the dying process, the withdrawing energies move away from the extremities of the physical body towards the appropriate door of exit and become focussed in the area around that door for the final "pull" of the directing soul.[10]

Chapter 2 discussed three methods that could help a dying person pass through the transition of death with full consciousness: use of sounds, color, and homeopathy. There is a fourth method. The enumeration in the formula's last sentence refers to the major chakras, where the "first" is the crown and the "seventh" is the basic. The blending of the will radiation with the crown chakra could help the patient to focus the withdrawing energies in the area around that chakra during the dying process. If such focussing were to occur, the withdrawing energies would pass up the spine, sequentially stimulating all major chakras except for the lowest one ("and re-establish thus the fifth, the third, the first, but not the seventh"), before the energies were finally released from the opening or exit at the top of the head. As a result, the patient would experience success in the final act of physical life, an illumination similar to *samadhi*—which is a Sanskrit word that means "self-aware conscious union with Spirit"—and a conscious passing to the after-death state.[11]

---

[10] Bailey, *A Treatise on White Magic*, pp. 496-504; Bailey, *Esoteric Healing*, pp. 472-478.

[11] A. A. Bailey, *Esoteric Psychology*, vol. 2 (1942; reprint; New York: Lucis Publishing Company, 1981), p. 66.

Ray Two

Let the healing energy descend, carrying its dual lines of life and its magnetic force. Let that magnetic living force withdraw and supplement that which is present in the seventh, opposing four and six to three and seven, but dealing not with five. The circular, inclusive vortex—descending to the point—disturbs, removes and then supplies and thus the work is done.

The heart revolves; two hearts revolve as one; the twelve within the vehicle, the twelve within the head and the twelve upon the plane of soul endeavor, cooperate as one and thus the work is done. Two energies achieve this consummation and the three whose number is a twelve respond to the greater twelve. The life is known and the years prolonged.[12]

Before discussing the second-ray formula, it may be helpful to provide some background information. The Sanskrit word *prana* is derived from *pra,* which means "forth," and the verb root *an,* which means "to breathe." Thus, *prana* means "to breathe forth," and it refers to the "life breath" or "life force" that vitalizes the etheric body and nervous system. Bailey characterized prana as "active radiatory heat."[13] Franz Anton Mesmer discovered this energy in 1774 and named it "animal magnetism."[14] Yogi Ramacharaka gave the following definition: "Prana is the Force by which all activity is carried on in the body—by which

---

[12] Bailey, *Esoteric Healing,* pp. 707, 708.

[13] A. A. Bailey, *A Treatise on Cosmic Fire* (1925; reprint; New York: Lucis Publishing Company, 1977), p. 102.

[14] H. F. Ellenberger, *The Discovery of the Unconscious* (New York: Basic Books, 1970), p. 59.

all bodily movements are possible—by which all functioning is done—by which all signs of life manifest themselves."[15]

Prana is neither mental nor emotional in nature, but it is the substance of which the planetary etheric body is made. As generally understood, prana exists in the atmosphere and enters the human etheric body by way of the splenic chakra, which is the etheric counterpart of the dense physical organ. Because the splenic chakra is a minor chakra, Table 1 (on page 16) does not list it as one of the seven major chakras. After passing through the splenic chakra, the prana circulates throughout the human etheric body and a portion is assimilated by each major chakra. Charles W. Leadbeater published a detailed description of this process of absorbing and assimilating prana, and he indicated that his description was based on his own clairvoyant observations.[16]

According to Bailey, prana varies in vibration and quality depending on the receiving chakra. As discussed in chapter 2, each chakra has a rate of vibration that may or may not be the same as its true natural frequency. After being assimilated by any chakra, the prana takes on the vibratory rate of that chakra. Because there are seven major chakras, there are seven principal forms of pranic energy in the etheric body— each form having the vibratory rate of a major chakra. In addition, the prana in a chakra acquires the quality of the various forces acting there. Because the chakras are focussing points for all interior forces, the assimilated prana could be affected or conditioned by forces coming from the emotional body, mental body, and soul.[17]

---

[15] Yogi Ramacharaka, *The Science of Psychic Healing* (1909; reprint; Chicago: Yogi Publication Society, 1937), p. 37.

[16] Bailey, *A Treatise on White Magic*, pp. 285, 433; C. W. Leadbeater, *The Chakras* (1927; reprint; Wheaton, IL: Theosophical Publishing House, 1977), pp. 53-70.

[17] Bailey, *A Treatise on Cosmic Fire*, pp. 99, 102; Bailey, *Esoteric Healing*, pp. 275, 627.

Although we cannot see prana out in the atmosphere with normal faculties, we can sense the presence of prana within us as a feeling of vitality and aliveness. Prana is the energy that is transmitted in what is sometimes called "laying-on-of-hands healing," and a recipient can often sense the impact of the transmitted energy as a tingling or subtle pressure on the skin. In laboratory experiments, scientists have shown that transmitting this energy has measurable effects on mice, plants,[18] enzyme growth,[19] and water.[20]

This section describes a method of pranic healing that is based upon knowledge of the chakras. The approach is to identify a chakra in the patient's etheric body that needs treatment and then to send a stream of prana to that chakra. As indicated by the preceding discussion, the frequency and quality of the transmitted prana depend upon the chakra from which it comes. Because the patient's chakra may be receptive to prana coming from only the corresponding chakra in the healer's etheric body, the healer's effort should be to send prana from there. Bailey also makes the last point: "The concept in the mind of the healer should be . . . that an unimpeded channel or a clear passage must be formed along which health-giving life may flow from the 'needed centre' in the healer's etheric body to the allied centre in the body of the patient."[21]

It is important to remember that the etheric body is part of the physical realm. Just as the conscious mind can direct the movements of the dense physical body, the mind can also

---

[18] B. Grad, "Laboratory Evidence of the 'Laying-on-of-Hands'" in *The Dimensions of Healing: A Symposium* (Los Altos, CA: Academy of Parapsychology and Medicine, 1972), pp. 29-34.

[19] Sister M. J. Smith, "The Influence of Enzyme Growth by the 'Laying-on-of-Hands,'" *The Dimensions of Healing: A Symposium*, pp. 110-120.

[20] R. N. Miller, "Methods of Detecting and Measuring Healing Energies" in *Future Science*, eds., J. White and S. Krippner (Garden City, NY: Anchor-Doubleday, 1977), pp. 431-444.

[21] Bailey, *Esoteric Healing*, pp. 626, 627.

direct the energy movements of the etheric physical body. As Bailey repeatedly emphasizes, "energy follows thought."[22] Thus, a healer can send currents of prana to the patient simply by using directed thought and the power of visualization. As discussed later in this section, however, the movement of prana is physically restricted by the roles of the chakras and their development.

The second-ray formula describes a method of healing in which the transmitted prana has the second-ray quality, namely, the love-wisdom of the monad. As shown in Table 7 (on page 112), love-wisdom can reach the heart and solar plexus chakras, which can then affect the sacral and basic chakras. Thus, this method of pranic healing is appropriate when treating the heart chakra or any lower chakra of the patient. The fifth and seventh sections of this chapter describe methods of pranic healing that are appropriate when treating the other major chakras.

Let us now consider the first sentence in the first paragraph. Mentally direct the descent of healing energy from your etheric body to that of the patient ("Let the healing energy descend"). This energy includes two different streams of life energy that are closely related ("carrying its dual lines of life"): the life stream and prana. The life stream emanates from the monad, passes through the soul, and is anchored in the heart chakra. Prana is absorbed from the atmosphere via the splenic chakra and then circulates throughout the etheric body. The life stream keeps the physical body coherent, and it controls the circulation of prana in the etheric body as well as the circulation of blood in the dense physical body. On the other hand, prana vitalizes the individual atoms and cells. In addition to the life stream and prana, the healing energy carries the second-ray quality of love-wisdom ("and its magnetic force").[23]

The second sentence gives a clue to a major cause of disease, and its enumeration refers to the seven planes as illustrated in figure 1 (on page 3). The urge to express one's higher

[22] Bailey, *Esoteric Healing,* p. 575.
[23] Bailey, *Esoteric Healing,* pp. 428, 429.

nature may be resisted by one's lower nature. This resistance may localize itself in some area of the physical body and produce a point of friction. If the personality focuses on the point of friction and *resents* the perceived inadequacy, then that point becomes an area of inflammation that may eventually turn into disease. For instance, group consciousness comes from the fourth (or buddhic) plane and may be resisted by self-centered feelings on the sixth (or emotional) plane. Group consciousness is received via the heart chakra, and friction occurs when the solar plexus chakra fails to express the corresponding feelings. Altruistic motivations emanate from the third (or atmic) plane and may be resisted by compulsive, self-centered behavior on the seventh (or physical) plane. Altruistic motivations are experienced via the crown chakra, and friction occurs when any of the lower chakras fails to be obedient and reacts compulsively to outer conditions. An abstract or spiritual principle comes from the fifth (or mental) plane and may be resisted by limiting beliefs that are also on the fifth plane. A principle is perceived via the brow chakra, and friction occurs when the throat chakra fails to express thoughts and speech embodying that principle. Thus, from this point of view, the three aspects of one's higher nature may produce disease in the physical body.[24]

Any method of pranic healing treats only the etheric effects, not the underlying conflicts. Thus, it can abate a disease but not bring about a permanent cure. The type of healing energy considered in this section can remove and replace the etheric effects ("Let that magnetic living force withdraw and supplement that which is present in the seventh") of two inner conflicts: group consciousness opposing self-centered feelings ("opposing four and six") or altruistic motivations opposing compulsive behavior ("to three and seven"), but not abstract principles opposing limiting beliefs ("but dealing not with five"). The etheric effects of the last conflict can be alleviated by using the methods described in the fifth and seventh sections of this chapter.[25]

---

[24] Bailey, *Esoteric Healing,* pp. 564-569.
[25] Bailey, *Esoteric Healing,* p. 329.

By using the power of thought, create a focal point of con-centrated attention that becomes the directing agent for the healing force or prana ("The circular inclusive vortex"). After absorbing as much prana as possible from the atmosphere, men-tally direct it to and through the appropriate chakra belong-ing to the patient ("descending to the point"). Each hand contains a chakra—one of the twenty-one minor chakras in the etheric body—and you can use your hand chakras to help focus the prana right at the patient's chakra. After reaching that chakra, the healing energy disturbs, removes, and then replaces the diseased vital energy of the patient ("disturbs, removes and then supplies"). Thus, pranic healing might be regarded as a sys-tem of *flushing* with a purificatory and stimulating effect ("and thus the work is done").[26]

Before interpreting the second paragraph, let us con-sider the meaning of its symbols. As discussed in the second section of chapter 2, the word *heart* can refer to either the heart chakra or soul. Table 1 (on page 16) lists the number of petals for each etheric chakra and shows that this number is a mul-tiple of twelve for either the crown, brow, or heart chakra. The number of petals for the soul (or egoic lotus) is also twelve. Thus, the word *twelve* can refer to the crown chakra, brow chakra, heart chakra, or soul.

The second paragraph describes how you can produce the healing energy. For the first step, definitely and consciously link up with your own soul; this enables it to be the controlling and directing agency for the process that follows ("The heart revolves"). With this alignment, you can receive wisdom from your soul and also guidance from your spirit guide or Master on the inner planes. Such guidance is conveyed intuitively through the soul, a process described in chapter 2.

For the second step, bring the love-wisdom of the monad down through your soul and heart chakra, which enables these two centers to be related and synchronized ("two hearts

---

[26] Bailey, *Esoteric Healing*, p. 287.

revolve as one"). This step is equivalent to experiencing compassion, and it is described in more detail in the fourth-ray section of this chapter.

For the third step, bring love-wisdom down to your solar plexus chakra. According to Bailey, "the solar plexus centre is awakened by the inflow of energy of a dual nature—the energies of the heart and the head, working synchronously."[27] Thus, the effort here is to create and sustain a triangle of force between the following three centers: your heart chakra ("the twelve within the vehicle"), which focuses the energy of love-wisdom; your crown or head chakra ("the twelve within the head"), which focuses the energy of will and has the power of directing the activities of the lower chakras; and your soul ("and the twelve upon the plane of soul endeavor"), which conveys the energy of will to the crown chakra and the energy of love-wisdom to the heart chakra. The cooperation of these centers enables your solar plexus chakra to awaken with love-wisdom ("cooperate as one and thus the work is done"). This step is equivalent to cultivating the feeling of positive regard, and it is described in more detail in the sixth-ray section of this chapter.[28]

The forces in the lowest three chakras control the personality. The solar plexus chakra is the focal point for feelings and desires. The sacral chakra governs the sexual life and organs of reproduction. The basic chakra feeds the fundamental instinct of self-preservation to all parts of the physical body. These three centers form an interrelated triangle of energy. Due to this interrelationship, the awakening of the solar plexus chakra affects the other two chakras. Thus, the first three steps enable love-wisdom to transmit its quality to the prana in the heart, solar plexus, sacral, and basic chakras.[29]

---

[27] Bailey, *Discipleship in the New Age,* vol. 2, p. 122.

[28] Bailey, *Esoteric Healing,* pp. 696-698.

[29] A. A. Bailey, *Initiation, Human and Solar* (1922; reprint; New York: Lucis Publishing Company, 1974), p. 204; Bailey, *Esoteric Healing,* pp. 169-189.

For the fourth step, consciously control the activity of the "needed center" and gather its prana into the brow chakra. Here, the needed center is the chakra in your etheric body that corresponds to the patient's chakra that you wish to treat. To accomplish this step, it is necessary to create another triangle of force between the following centers: the crown chakra, where the consciousness stream is anchored; the heart chakra, where the life stream is anchored; and the brow (or ajna) chakra, the temporary custodian of the pranic energy. The consciousness stream can direct the life stream, which in turn controls the circulation of prana.

Keep aligned with the soul, receive the energy of will from the soul, hold your consciousness steady in the crown chakra, and turn your "eye of direction" toward the needed center. The consciousness stream includes the powers of thought, imagination, and will. By using the powers of this stream, channel the energy of will into the needed center and bring that chakra under rhythmic control. The goal here is to ensure that the chakra is vibrating at its natural and normal frequency. This phase of the technique is the same as the last portion of the instruction given in the seventh-ray method of chapter 2. Next, by using the powers of the consciousness stream, direct the life stream so that it carries the prana from the needed center to the brow chakra. Thus, the two streams working together complete the preparation of the healing energy ("Two energies achieve this consummation"), and the second triangle of force responds to the guidance and direction of the soul ("and the three whose number is a twelve respond to the greater twelve").

The first and fourth steps are general and also apply to the methods of pranic healing discussed later in this chapter. The second and third steps are more specific and assume that the needed center is one of the four lowest chakras. The primary triangle defined in the third step affects the healer, and it enables the prana in the needed center to have the quality of love-wisdom. The secondary triangle defined in the fourth step produces the effect upon the patient and is the one through which the healer works on the physical plane. Because the energy of will is the first subray of the soul ray, the initial portion of the fourth step relates the soul ray to the needed center. Bailey describes the entire fourth step in the following way:

> The healer, having aligned himself with the soul and "tapped" soul energy (thereby making himself a channel for spiritual force), directs this energy into that one of his own centres which corresponds to the centre conditioning the area of the point of friction . . . .This radiation [passes] through two stages: 1) The stage wherein the soul radiated energy into the head centre. 2) The stage wherein the healer directs a ray of that energy from the head centre into the "needed centre."[30]

> He will next create the secondary triangle by focussing his attention in the centre of receptivity, the head center. He will then connect this head centre, through the power of the creative imagination, with the centre between the eyebrows, and will hold the energy there because it is the directing agency. He will endeavor to gather into this ajna centre the energy of that centre within his etheric body which is related to his soul ray.[31]

For the fifth and final step, send the pranic energy from your brow chakra, through your hand chakras, to the appropriate chakra belonging to the patient. With this effort, the patient experiences greater vitality and a prolonged period of physical health ("The life is known and the years prolonged"). Bailey gives this description:

---

[30] Bailey, *Esoteric Healing,* pp. 602-604.
[31] Bailey, *Esoteric Healing,* p. 698.

When the karma or life-pattern of the patient permits, these energy rays (emanating from the magnetic field in the healer's head) become what is called a "dispelling radiance"; they can drive away the forces which create or aggravate the disease.[32]

Using the ajna centre as a distributing centre, [the healer] then uses his hands as the agency through which the directed energy can reach that area in the patient's body where the seat of the trouble is to be found. . . .The hands are laid on the centre in spine or head which may govern that area—the right hand being laid upon the spinal centre and the left hand on the part of the body immediately in front of the special area and over the part of the abdomen, chest or head in which the patient complains of distress.[33]

Only an advanced healer could apply the foregoing method because the third initiation is a prerequisite for using the brow chakra to direct and distribute prana, at least according to our understanding.[34] Douglas Baker seems to confirm this point of view: "It is only when the initiate takes his Third Degree that this planetary force can be consciously contacted and used with studied effect."[35]

Nevertheless, an average healer has the capacity to perform pranic healing. The reason is that prana can be distrib-

---

[32] Bailey, *Esoteric Healing,* pp. 580, 581.

[33] Bailey, *Esoteric Healing,* pp. 648, 649.

[34] Nowhere does Bailey clearly state that the third initiation is a prerequisite for using the brow chakra to distribute prana. However, she seems to imply this prerequisite in several locations: *Esoteric Healing,* pp. 580, 581; *A Treatise on Cosmic Fire,* p. 859; *A Treatise on White Magic,* p. 290; and *Discipleship in the New Age,* vol. 1 (1944; reprint; New York: Lucis Publishing Company, 1976), p. 28.

[35] Douglas Baker, *Esoteric Healing,* part I (High Road, Essendon, Herts., England: Dr. Douglas Baker, 1975), p. 202.

uted by two other chakras: the splenic and solar plexus chakras, which are fully developed in an average person. The prana distributed by the splenic chakra, however, comes from only that chakra, so it carries the vibratory frequency and quality of the splenic chakra. Similarly, the prana distributed by the solar plexus chakra comes from only that chakra, so it carries the frequency and quality of the solar plexus chakra. Thus, an average healer is able to treat only illnesses that are responsive to these two types of prana, primarily diseases found below the diaphragm. But by working through the brow chakra, an advanced healer can extract prana from any major chakra and then direct that energy via the brow to the allied center in the patient.[36]

Ray Three

The healer stands and weaves. He gathers from the three, the five, the seven that which is needed for the heart of life. He brings the energies together and makes them serve the third; he thus creates a vortex into which the one distressed must descend and with him goes the healer. And yet they both remain in peace and calm. Thus must the angel of the Lord descend into the pool and bring the healing life.[37]

The third-ray formula describes how the active intelligence of the monad can be radiated as part of the aura. The basic approach is to carry out the stages of raja yoga that were presented in the fifth-ray section of chapter 3. The third column of Table 7 (on page 112) outlines the line of transmission for this process, showing both the vertical and horizontal relationships.

[36] Z. F Lansdowne, *The Chakras and Esoteric Healing* (York Beach, ME: Samuel Weiser, 1986), pp. 60-62; Bailey, *Esoteric Healing,* pp. 578-580.
[37] Bailey, *Esoteric Healing,* p. 708.

Let us consider the first sentence in the above formula. By progressing through the concentration, meditation, and contemplation stages of raja yoga, you can raise temporarily the center of your consciousness into the next higher aspect of your inner self—namely, that aspect lying just above your normal awareness ("The healer stands"). This next higher aspect might be the soul, the spiritual triad, or even the monad. No matter where your center normally lies, some aspect is always still higher and is beckoning you. Through raising the focal point of your consciousness, you receive new ideas and have new perspectives ("and weaves"). Bailey says, "As man the human being, man the disciple, and man the initiate gradually move onward on the stream of life, revelation comes step by step, moving from one great point of focus to another."[38]

Next, you enter the illumination stage and gather some or all of the following elements: revelations from the active intelligence of the monad, the third-ray quality ("He gathers from the three"); insights from the spiritual mind, wisdom from the soul, and concrete thoughts from the mental body, all on the fifth or mental plane ("the five"); and facts and symbols from the brain on the seventh or physical plane ("the seven"). Use whatever elements are needed for converting your new ideas into a deeper understanding regarding the meaning and purpose of life ("that which is needed for the heart of life"). For instance, contrast your ideas with alternative ones, relate the facts of the material world to your ideas, or learn how your ideas can be applied in a practical way.

If you have achieved the third initiation, then you can make direct contact with the active intelligence of the monad and receive revelations from there. Bailey points out the difficulty of describing what those revelations convey:

> When we come, therefore, to the great organ of universal revelation, the monadic principle, functioning

---

[38] Bailey, *Discipleship in the New Age*, vol. 2, p. 293.

through the medium of an extra-planetary light, we enter realms which are indefinable and for which no terminology has been created, and which only initiates above the third degree are able to consider.[39]

If you have not achieved the third initiation, you can still make indirect contact with the active intelligence by receiving insights from the spiritual mind. In either case, use the revelations or insights to guide the wisdom of the soul, which you then can use to guide the thoughts of the mind, which in turn controls the activity of the brain ("He brings the energies together").

When you integrate the foregoing elements, you also bring the active intelligence of the monad down to the physical plane where it affects the activity of your throat chakra, the third chakra listed in Table 1 (on page 16) ("and makes them serve the third"). As a result, your throat chakra radiates an aura of mental strength and clarity into which the patient must enter when he or she is present with you ("he thus creates a vortex into which the one distressed must descend and with him goes the healer"). If the patient is an ordinary or average person and is properly receptive, then his or her throat chakra will respond to the mental emanations of your aura.[40]

You gain mental strength and clarity through entering the illumination stage of raja yoga and furthering your understanding of life. Because the patient gains the same qualities through contact with your aura, both your mind and the patient's mind become peaceful and calm ("And yet they both remain in peace and calm"). If the mental attitude is sufficiently strengthened, then it will control emotional reactions. In this case, the peace and calm of the patient's mind will descend into his or her emotional body, bringing dispassion and quiet to the emotional nature ("Thus must the angel of the Lord descend into the pool and bring the healing life").

---

[39] Bailey, *Discipleship in the New Age,* vol. 2, p. 294.
[40] Bailey, *Esoteric Healing,* pp. 551, 656.

The four methods of radiatory healing discussed in this chapter differ in several respects: the quality of the radiation, the chakras used for transmission and reception, the development required in the healer and patient, and the effects on the patient. Although each method is being presented separately, an advanced healer might well accomplish all four methods simultaneously. Through any or all methods, a healer is able to uplift and strengthen people without having to speak. Meher Baba describes this circumstance in the following way:

> The ancient Rishis have attached great importance to having the darshana of saints and masters, because they are the source of the constant flow of love and light which emanates from them and makes an irresistible appeal to the inner feeling of the aspirant even when he receives no verbal instruction from them. The effect of the darshana is dependent upon the receptivity and response of the aspirant.[41]

In the above passage, the Sanskrit word *rishis* means "sages," and the word *darshana* can be translated as "holy sight."

Ray Four

The healer knows the place where dissonance is found. He also knows the power of sound and the sound which must be heard. Knowing the note to which the fourth great group reacts and linking it to the great Creative Nine, he sounds the note which brings release, the note which will bring absorption into one.

---

[41] M. Baba, *Discourses,* vol. 2 (San Francisco: Sufism Reoriented, 1967), p. 93.

He educates the listening ear of him who must be healed;
he likewise trains the listening ear of him who must
go forth. He knows the manner of the sound which
brings the healing touch; and also that which says:
Depart. And thus the work is done.[42]

The fourth-ray formula describes another type of radiatory healing. Here, the love-wisdom of the monad descends
to the heart chakra and radiates outwardly from there. The second column of Table 7 (on page 112) provides an outline for
this process.

The first portion of the formula indicates the knowledge
needed to accomplish this method of healing. First, know
that conflicts between human beings occur only at the level
of the personality, not at the higher levels of the human constitution ("The healer knows the place where dissonance is found").
As shown in figure 1 (on page 3), the higher levels include the
monad, spiritual triad, and soul.

Second, know that the love-wisdom of the monad has
the power to heal any conflict that might rise ("He also knows
the power of sound") and that it is the source of all varieties
of love that occur within the human constitution. But this
quality can resolve conflicts only when it is brought down into
the personality from the higher levels.

Third, to bring love-wisdom down, you must intuitively sense
the presence of God throughout the universe in all bodily forms
("and the sound which must be heard"). In other words, you
must "isolate the germ or seed of divinity which has brought
all forms into being."[43] It is not the vision of the soul that must
be sensed, but what the light of the soul can aid in revealing.
The necessary approach is to release yourself from all emotional
and mental ties, learn to follow the will of the soul, and then

---

[42] Bailey, *Esoteric Healing*, p. 709.

[43] A. A. Bailey, *Glamour: A World Problem* (1950; reprint; New York: Lucis Publishing
Company, 1971), p. 180.

learn to function as the soul. After you have reached union with the soul, even if only temporarily, the light of the soul can become focussed and intuitively reveal the vision of the presence.

For instance, you might have the following series of intuitive realizations. Your true identity is consciousness, awareness, or spiritual reality. Because this identity lies beyond all mental self-images of personal pride and guilt, you did not create your *self*. Although your mind can create self-images and can deceive itself by believing in their reality, you are the consciousness that perceives those images. Because you were created perfectly by God and remain as you were created, you remain pure, sinless, and holy. The belief that you did create your self is the root of all your problems. Accepting God as your source or creator establishes your peace of mind. The source of your life is also the source of all lives.[44]

The intuitive perception of the presence of God is sometimes called spiritual love. Evoking this perception can be thought of as bringing the love-wisdom of the monad down to the buddhic plane, enabling you to make indirect contact with that quality. Your experience of spiritual love will probably be dim and faint, but after having it you can clearly and strongly experience compassion, the intuition of the essential nonseparateness and equality of all human beings. Evoking compassion can be thought of as bringing love-wisdom down to the mental plane, the level of the soul, enabling you to perceive the unity of all souls.

In the third sentence of the formula, the "fourth great group" refers to the heart chakra, because it is the fourth one listed in Table 1 (on page 16), and the "great Creative Nine" refers to the nine outer petals of the egoic lotus that are described in Table 6 (on page 90). Compassion is the energy to which the heart chakra reacts and that links it with the egoic lotus— the soul ("Knowing the note to which the fourth great group

---

[44] *A Course in Miracles,* vol. 1 (Tiburon, CA: Foundation for Inner Peace, 1975), pp. 43-46.

reacts and linking it to the great Creative Nine"). By having compassion, you can radiate this energy from your heart chakra ("he sounds the note"). If the patient is sufficiently developed and receptive, then his or her heart chakra will respond to the emanations of compassion in your aura. As a result, the patient will be released from a sense of separation and will experience a oneness with humanity ("which brings release, the note which will bring absorption into one").

The rest of the symbolic formula describes the effects of this type of radiatory healing. As discussed in the second section of this chapter, a chakra has an associated quality and rate of vibration, both of which can be conveyed through the healer's aura. First, let us consider the effect of radiating the quality of compassion. People can respond to this quality only if they have begun the process of becoming aware of love's presence within themselves. One group that can respond consists of people who have made progress on the spiritual path and have already felt the oneness of humanity, but who have succumbed to a temporary condition of emotional self-centeredness. For such people, the effect of radiating compassion is to help them regain their earlier point of attainment, which they must do before they can make any further progress ("He educates the listening ear of him who must be healed"). Beginners on the spiritual path can also respond. In their case, the effect of the radiation is to encourage them to go forth on the path of probation, which they must do to unfold their spiritual nature ("he likewise trains the listening ear of him who must go forth").

The radiation of the heart chakra also can produce beneficial physical effects. As discussed in the seventh section of chapter 2 (see page 62), physical disease can occur when the vibratory rate of a chakra deviates from its true natural frequency. Through the vibratory field of your aura, you can establish a resonant system between your heart chakra and that of the patient, which brings the vibratory rate of the patient's chakra back to its own natural frequency ("He knows the manner of the sound which brings the healing touch"). Because a dense physical disorder is only a symptom of an etheric disorder, restoring right rhythm on the etheric level will also cause ill-health to depart from an associated organ on the dense physical level ("and also that which says: Depart").

In summary, love-wisdom can radiate through the heart chakra and do the following: salvage travellers on the spiritual path, encourage others to move forward on that path, restore balance to the etheric body, and remove ill-health from the dense physical body ("And thus the work is done"). The basic characteristic of the fourth ray is unification. Because the heart radiation produces unity and harmony among human beings and within the physical body, it can be thought of as expressing the fourth subray of love-wisdom. *A Course in Miracles* seems to describe this type of radiatory healing:

> The peace of God is shining in you now, and from your heart extends around the world. It pauses to caress each living thing, and leaves a blessing with it that remains forever and forever. What it gives must be eternal. It removes all thoughts of the ephemeral and valueless. It brings renewal to all tired hearts, and lights all vision as it passes by.[45]

Bailey describes it as follows:

> [The aspirant] will then become a channel for the light of the Ego, for the illumination of buddhi to pour through for the saving of the race, and the lighting of those who stumble in dark places. . . . His life must begin to radiate, and to have a magnetic effect upon others. By this I mean he will begin to influence that which is imprisoned in others, for he will reach— through his own powerful vibrations—the hidden cen-

---

[45] *A Course in Miracles,* vol. 2, p. 347.

tre in each one. . . . I refer to that spiritual radiation that is only responded to and realised by those who themselves are becoming aware of the spiritual centre within the heart. At this stage the man is recognised as one who can speak occultly "heart to heart." He becomes a stimulator of the heart centre in his brother, and one who arouses men into activity for others.[46]

Ray Five

That which has been given must be used; that which emerges from within the given mode will find its place within the healer's plan. That which is hidden must be seen and from the three, great knowledge will emerge. For these the healer seeks. To these the healer adds the two which are as one, and so the fifth must play its part and the five must play its part and the five must function as if one. The energies descend, pass through and disappear, leaving the one who could respond with karma yet to dissipate and taking with them him who may not thus respond and so must likewise disappear.[47]

The fifth-ray formula describes the method of pranic healing in which the active intelligence of the monad conveys its quality to the transmitted prana. As shown in Table 7 (on page 112), the active intelligence can pass through the inner human constitution and reach the throat chakra in the etheric body. Thus, this method is appropriate when treating that particular chakra.

---

[46] Bailey, *A Treatise on Cosmic Fire,* p. 863.
[47] Bailey, *Esoteric Healing,* p. 710.

Before implementing any method of pranic healing, Bailey recommends that the healer spend a minimum of five hours of quiet thought to diagnose the patient's disease. The following issues are investigated during this period: "a) The problem of the disease and its particular nature; b) Its location in the physical body; c) The chakra involved and . . . its condition; d) The acuteness of the difficulty and the chance of a cure; e) The danger of death or not; f) The psychological condition of the patient; g) The rays of the patient."[48]

The initial portion of the formula describes this preliminary step. The active intelligence of the monad has been given to you by the planetary Logos, and you must use that quality to arrive at an accurate diagnosis ("That which has been given must be used").[49] The necessary approach is to apply the stages of raja yoga discussed in the fifth-ray section (page 95) of chapter 3. Thus, begin with the stages of concentration and meditation on each of the seven issues listed above. If you achieve the advanced stages of raja yoga, you will be a successful healer because you will seldom make mistakes. The spiritual mind's insights and the soul's wisdom emerge from within the contemplation stage, bringing the active intelligence down to the abstract levels of the mental plane ("that which emerges from within the given mode will find its place within the healer's plan"). The insights and wisdom, being abstract in nature, must be converted by the mental body into a concrete treatment plan during the illumination stage ("That which is hidden must be seen"). Because this mental effort requires alignment with the third or throat chakra, the active intelligence will emerge from there ("and from the three, great knowledge will emerge"). As a result, you will arrive at an accurate understanding of what to do, and the active intelligence will affect the prana in your throat chakra ("For these the healer seeks").

---

[48] Bailey, *Esoteric Healing*, p. 702.
[49] A. A. Bailey, *Initiation, Human and Solar* (1922; reprint; New York: Lucis Publishing Company, 1974), pp. 117, 118.

Diagnosis implies discriminating between those chakras that need treatment and those that do not need attention. Correct discrimination requires the activity of the fifth-ray quality of the soul, which in this case is the fifth subray of the monadic quality of active intelligence. The next portion of the formula assumes that the patient's throat chakra has been diagnosed as needing treatment with prana, and it reviews some of the information given during the discussion of the second-ray formula.

To the active intelligence you must add the two streams of life energy that are closely related: the life stream and prana ("To these the healer adds the two which are as one"). Thus, several elements have roles in this method. The fifth or mental plane must play its part by transmitting the active intelligence through the spiritual mind, soul, and mental body ("and so the fifth must play its part"). The following five chakras must also play their part: splenic, heart, throat, brow, and crown ("and the five must play its part"). The splenic chakra absorbs prana from the atmosphere. The life stream is anchored in the heart chakra, and it controls the circulation of prana. Some prana is raised to the throat chakra where it acquires the frequency of that chakra and the quality of the active intelligence. The throat prana is raised to the brow chakra and from there is distributed to the patient. The consciousness stream is anchored in the crown chakra, and it can direct the life stream. You must ensure that these five chakras function in a coordinated and integrated way ("and the five must function as if one").

Healing work is circulatory. When mentally sending prana to the patient's throat chakra, do not visualize or think of the prana as accumulating there. Rather, visualize the descending prana as passing through the chakra, entering the diseased organ or the area where the disease is located, and then moving out to the body as a whole ("The energies descend, pass through and disappear"). This process leaves new prana that has the right frequency and quality for healthful activity, and it flushes out the earlier prana that was not healthful and that needed to be removed ("leaving the one who could respond with karma yet to dissipate and taking with them him who may not thus respond and so must likewise disappear").[50]

Ray Six

Cleaving the waters, let the power descend, the healer cries. He minds not how the waters may respond; they oft bring stormy waves and dire and dreadful happenings. The end is good. The trouble will be ended when the storm subsides and energy has fulfilled its charted destiny. Straight to the heart the power is forced to penetrate, and into every channel, nadi, nerve and spleen the power must seek a passage and a way and thus confront the enemy who has effected entrance and settled down to live. Ejection—ruthless, sudden and complete—is undertaken by the one who sees naught else but perfect functioning and brooks no interference. This perfect functioning opens thus the door to life eternal or to life on earth for yet a little while.[51]

As outlined in the second column of Table 7 (on page 112), love-wisdom can radiate through both the heart and solar plexus chakras. The fourth-ray formula describes the process and effects of radiating this quality through the heart chakra, and the sixth-ray formula gives the corresponding description for the solar plexus chakra.

In this fourth and final type of radiatory healing, your first step is eliminating your own negative feelings such as resentment, criticism, and envy ("Cleaving the waters"). As discussed in the sixth-ray section (page 100) of chapter 3, emotional reac-

---

[50] Bailey, *Esoteric Healing*, p. 287.
[51] Bailey, *Esoteric Healing*, p. 711.

tions originate in the beliefs and opinions held by the mind. Therefore, rather than struggling with or trying to suppress your negative feelings, it is more effective to change your thoughts. The following are some brief rules that can aid in making the needed mental change. Observe the contents of the mind, and work consciously at purifying the mind of all prejudices, preconceived ideas, and hasty judgments. Practice harmlessness in thought and word. And refuse to think unkindly or with criticism regarding the patient for whom you plan to work.[52]

The second step of the technique is actually a continuation of the fourth-ray method: make an effort to perceive the presence of God in all forms, including that of the patient. If this effort is successful, the love-wisdom of the monad can descend to the buddhic level in the form of spiritual love and to the soul level in the form of compassion. If you are able to eliminate enough of your negative feelings during the first step, then the love-wisdom can descend further and reach your emotional body in the form of positive regard ("let the power descend"), which is a feeling of acceptance, appreciation, and respect for the patient. Nonetheless, maintaining this feeling requires a definite and sustained effort ("the healer cries").

You have a basic choice of how to perceive the patient. If you look with the intuitive perception of your soul, then you will perceive that person as a spiritual being who has been created perfectly by God and remains uncorrupted, leading to the feeling of unconditional positive regard. But if you look with the eyes of your personality, you will have judgments, evaluations, and assessments, leading to negative or critical feelings. In practice, you may fluctuate from one type of perception to the other.

As love-wisdom descends into the emotional body, you may experience a conflict between it and any negative feelings that might still remain there. In this case, you should not place any attention on the negative feelings or the conflict ("He

---

[52] Bailey, *Discipleship in the New Age*, vol. 1, pp. 65, 66.

minds not how the waters may respond"). For instance, you may have the feeling that the patient is not worthy of receiving the healing energy and that he or she should suffer guilt and be punished ("they oft bring stormy waves and dire and dreadful happenings"). Instead, remain devoted to perceiving the patient as unblemished spiritual reality, as pure consciousness that exists beyond but acts through the personality ("The end is good"). Devotion to a spiritual ideal is a sixth-ray ability. Because you are no longer feeding the old emotional patterns, they will eventually decay. Your emotional conflict will be ended when the negative feelings do subside and positive regard has replaced them ("The trouble will be ended when the storm subsides and energy has fulfilled its charted destiny").

The solar plexus chakra is exceedingly active for most people. This chakra is the outlet of the emotional body into the outer world, and it receives all emotional reactions and desire impulses. It is the dominant chakra within people who are approaching the spiritual path, and its control is a vital goal for aspirants on that path. The second section of chapter 3 introduced the concept of the solar Logos. According to Bailey, both the solar plexus chakra and the heart chakra are reflections in the personality of the heart center of the solar Logos.[53] Thus, in Bailey's symbolic formula, the word *heart* can be interpreted as referring to the solar plexus chakra.

When you experience positive regard for the patient, that feeling radiates from your solar plexus chakra and goes straight to the solar plexus chakra of the patient where it penetrates ("Straight to the heart the power is forced to penetrate"). In yoga philosophy, the Sanskrit word *nadi* refers to a subtle channel of energy that underlies and affects the nervous system. After positive regard enters the patient's solar plexus chakra, it passes into the associated etheric channels and nadis, the sympathetic nervous system, and the associated

[53] Bailey, *Esoteric Healing*, p. 170.

dense physical organs such as the liver, pancreas, stomach, and spleen ("and into every channel, nadi, nerve and spleen the power must seek a passage and a way"). Through this process, the radiation confronts the feelings of anxiety that have effected entrance into the patient and have become part of his or her emotional life ("and thus confront the enemy who has effected entrance and settled down to live").[54]

The love-wisdom radiation is able to eject the fearful reactions of the patient—in a prompt, sudden, and complete way—provided that you remain devoted to perceiving the patient as a perfect spiritual being and that you allow nothing to interfere with that attention ("Ejection—ruthless, sudden and complete—is undertaken by the one who sees naught else but perfect functioning and brooks no interference"). This emotional healing allows the patient to receive the wisdom of the soul and have better relationships with other people ("This perfect functioning opens thus the door to life eternal or to life on earth"). Because the improved condition will last for only a short period of time ("for yet a little while"), the patient needs to learn how love-wisdom can be evoked from within.

It is important to make the following distinction. This type of radiatory healing is able to remove fearful reactions from the patient, but it cannot directly remove painful feelings that have been repressed. Such feelings were denied awareness for being too threatening to the self-image that the patient wanted to maintain. Although the love-wisdom radiation can not remove those feelings, it can remove the patient's fear of them. By receiving unconditional acceptance from the healer, the patient gains the confidence needed to confront repressed material and to incorporate that material as part of a changing and developing self. As a result, the patient is helped in resolving inner contradictions and in unifying the personality.[55]

---

[54] Bailey, *Esoteric Healing* pp. 554, 555.

[55] C. R. Rogers, *On Becoming A Person* (Boston: Houghton Mifflin, 1961), p. 185.

Carl Rogers, one of the great innovators in modern psychology, emphasized the importance of cultivating the feeling of positive regard, and he described this feeling in the following way:

> It involves the therapist's genuine willingness for the client to be whatever feeling is going on in him at that moment—fear, confusion, pain, pride, anger, hatred, love, courage, or awe. It means that the therapist cares for the client, in a nonpossessive way. It means that he prizes the client in a total rather than a conditional way. By this I mean that he does not simply accept the client when he is behaving in certain ways, and disapprove of him when he behaves in other ways. It means an outgoing positive feeling without reservations, without evaluations. The term we have come to use for this is unconditional positive regard.[56]

Carl Rogers was a very effective therapist because he combined the sixth-ray method of esoteric healing with psychotherapy.

Ray Seven

Energy and force must meet each other and thus the work is done. Colour and sound in ordered sequence must meet and blend and thus the work of magic can proceed. Substance and spirit must evoke each other and, passing through the centre of the one who seeks to aid, produce the new and good. The healer energises thus with life the failing life, driving it forth or anchoring it yet more deeply in the place of des-

---

[56] Rogers, *On Becoming a Person*, p. 62.

tiny. All seven must be used and through the seven there must pass the energies the need requires, creating the new man who has for ever been and will for ever be, and either here or there.[57]

The seventh and final formula describes the method of pranic healing in which the monadic will conveys its quality to the transmitted prana. According to the first column in Table 7 (on page 112), the monadic will can reach both the crown and brow chakras within the etheric body. Thus, this method is appropriate when treating either of those chakras belonging to the patient.

One of the basic characteristics of the seventh ray is the ability to unify opposing forces. As shown in the first three sentences of the formula, the seventh-ray method of esoteric healing brings together three different pairs of opposites. The first pair is the healing prana and the diseased forces. When the stream of prana from your crown or brow chakra removes and replaces the diseased forces within the corresponding chakra of the patient, the healing work is accomplished ("Energy and force must meet each other and thus the work is done").

The second pair is prana and the monadic will. Because the seventh is the ray of ceremonial order or magic, the seventh-ray quality of the soul provides the ability to prepare and distribute prana. The method is to express the general monadic purpose of providing true service through the narrower seventh-ray purpose of transmitting appropriate prana, which brings the seventh subray of the monadic will down to your crown and brow chakras. As discussed in the second section of this chapter, prana enters the etheric body through the splenic chakra and then passes to the other chakras. After being assimilated by a given chakra, prana acquires the vibratory rate of that chakra and the quality of the forces acting there. When

---

[57] Bailey, *Esoteric Healing,* p. 712.

prana with the right frequency meets and blends with the monadic will within your crown or brow chakra, the work of healing can proceed with energy having the right frequency and quality ("Colour and sound in ordered sequence must meet and blend and thus the work of magic can proceed").

The third pair of energies is prana and the life stream. Prana provides the vitality that enables the physical body to evoke the life stream from the soul. On the other hand, the life stream controls the movement of prana and can evoke additional prana from the atmosphere. During the treatment, prana and the life stream must evoke each other and pass through the following sequence of centers ("Substance and spirit must evoke each other and, passing through the centre of the one who seeks to aid"): the center in your etheric body that corresponds to the one being treated in the patient; your brow chakra, which distributes the energy; and your hand chakras, which focus the energy. This process of distributing and focussing produces the stream of healing prana that is directed towards the patient ("produce the new and good").

Before discussing the remainder of the formula, it is necessary to introduce some additional concepts. An important correspondence exists between changes in consciousness and shifts of energy within the etheric body. For instance, when sexual or physical creativity is transmuted into artistic or mental creativity, the energy of the sacral chakra rises to the throat chakra. When self-centered desire is transmuted into group consciousness, the energy of the solar plexus chakra rises to the heart chakra. When material ambition is transmuted into a dedication to serve humanity, the energy of the basic chakra rises to the brow chakra. When the center of consciousness shifts from the personality to the soul, the energies of the heart and throat chakras rise to the brow chakra. And when the center of consciousness shifts to the spiritual triad, the energy of the brow chakra rises to the crown chakra.[58]

---

[58] Bailey, *Esoteric Healing*, p. 175; Bailey, *Esoteric Psychology*, vol. 2, pp. 523-527.

Your goal is to stimulate with prana the failing etheric body of the patient ("The healer energises thus with life the failing life"). After identifying the patient's chakra that governs the diseased area, determine whether the chakra is overactive or underactive. If the chakra is diagnosed as overactive, then drive away some of its energy ("driving it forth") by sending prana to stimulate the specific higher chakra that can potentially control it. In particular, a chakra can be controlled by the higher chakra that will eventually receive its energy, as listed in the preceding paragraph. On the other hand, if the chakra is diagnosed as underactive, then send prana there to intensify the life of that center ("or anchoring it yet more deeply in the place of destiny"). Bailey gives examples of these two types of treatment:

> [Healers] can, through the power of directed thought, pour energy into the centre which is the determining factor in that area of the physical body where the trouble lies. If, for instance, the patient is suffering from such a difficulty as gastric ulcer, the stimulation of the solar plexus centre may produce a cure.

> They can stimulate a centre higher than the one controlling a particular area and thus—by the intensification of the higher centre—reduce the vitality of the lower. If, for instance, there is disease or trouble in connection with the organs of generation (as for instance disease of the prostate gland), then the throat centre should receive attention. It is that centre which must eventually be the recipient of the energy of the lower creative aspect or correspondence. This is called the "technique of the withdrawal of the fire"; by its means what you call overstimulation in certain cases, or inflammation in others, can be stopped.[59]

---

[59] Bailey, *Esoteric Healing*, pp. 283, 284.

The foregoing instruction is meant to apply to all methods of pranic healing, yet its application can be considered within a particular method, such as the one using the brow and crown chakras. Prana is sent to the patient's brow chakra if that chakra is diagnosed as being underactive or if the heart, throat, or basic chakra is diagnosed as being overactive. And prana is sent to the patient's crown chakra if that chakra is diagnosed as being underactive or if the brow chakra is diagnosed as being overactive.

The final sentence of the formula shows how to contact the monadic will. The requisite effort can be described in three different ways: invocation, shifting the energies in the etheric body, or shifting the center of consciousness from one inner vehicle to another. The first-ray formula gives the first description and the seventh-ray formula gives the last two. These three descriptions are equivalent, because successful invocation requires shifting the energies in the etheric body and causes a shift in consciousness.

Your first step is merging the will of the personality with the sacrificial will of the soul. To accomplish this step, the energies of the five lowest chakras must pass into the brow chakra and become focussed there. As a result, the center of your consciousness shifts from the personality to the soul, which enables the energies of the soul to descend into the personality. Your next step is using the will of the soul-infused personality to invoke the will-to-good, the latter being the reflection of the monadic will on the level of the atmic plane. For a successful invocation, the energies of all seven major chakras must be used ("All seven must be used"), and those energies must pass through the seven chakras and become focussed in the crown chakra ("and through the seven there must pass the energies the need requires"). As a result, the center of your consciousness temporarily shifts to the spiritual triad ("creating the new man who has for ever been and will ever be"), enabling the monadic will to descend into the soul and personality ("and either here or there").[60] Bailey describes the experience of someone undergoing these shifts in consciousness:

> The disciple knows or is learning to know that he is not this or that, but Life Itself. He is not the physical body or its emotional nature; he is not . . . the mind or that by which he knows. He is learning that that too must be transcended and superseded by intelligent love (only truly possible after the mind has been developed), and he begins to realize himself as the soul. Then, later, comes the awful "moment in time" when, pendent in space, he discovers that he is not the soul. What then is he? A point of divine dynamic will, focussed in the soul and arriving at awareness of Being through the use of form. He is Will, the ruler of time and the organiser, in time, of space.[61]

In summary, the second-ray, fifth-ray, and seventh-ray formulas present information regarding various aspects of pranic healing, including both diagnosis and treatment. Because of their overlapping nature, one needs to understand the information in all three formulas before being ready to apply any of them.

---

[60] Bailey, *Esoteric Healing*, p. 188.
[61] Bailey, *The Rays and the Initiations*, p. 107.

BIBLIOGRAPHY

Assagioli, R. *Psychosynthesis.* 1965. Reprint. New York: Viking Penguin, 1987.

————. *Psychosynthesis Typology.* London: Institute of Psychosynthesis, 1983.

Baba, M. *Discourses.* San Francisco: Sufism Reoriented, 1967.

Bailey, A. A. *Discipleship in the New Age,* vol. 1. 1944. Reprint. New York: Lucis Publishing Company, 1976.

————. *Discipleship in the New Age,* vol. 2. 1955. Reprint. New York: Lucis Publishing Company, 1972.

————. *Education in the New Age.* 1954. Reprint. New York: Lucis Publishing Company, 1974.

————. *Esoteric Astrology.* 1951. Reprint. New York: Lucis Publishing Company, 1979.

————. *Esoteric Healing.* 1953. Reprint. New York: Lucis Publishing Company, 1977.

————. *Esoteric Psychology,* vol. 1. 1936. Reprint. New York: Lucis Publishing Company, 1975.

————. *Esoteric Psychology,* vol. 2. 1942. Reprint. New York: Lucis Publishing Company, 1975.

————. *The Externalisation of the Hierarchy.* 1957. Reprint. New York: Lucis Publishing Company, 1976.

————. *From Intellect to Intuition.* 1932. Reprint. New York: Lucis Publishing Company, 1974.

————. *Glamour: A World Problem.* 1950. Reprint. New York: Lucis Publishing Company, 1971.

————. *Initiation, Human and Solar.* 1922. Reprint. New York: Lucis Publishing Company, 1974.

————. *Letters on Occult Meditation.* 1922. Reprint. New York: Lucis Publishing Company, 1974.

————. *The Light of the Soul.* 1955. Reprint. New York: Lucis Publishing Company, 1978.

————. *The Rays and the Initiations.* 1960. Reprint. New York: Lucis Publishing Company, 1976.

————. *The Soul and Its Mechanism.* 1930. Reprint. New York: Lucis Publishing Company, 1976.

————. *Telepathy and the Etheric Vehicle.* 1950. Reprint. New York: Lucis Publishing Company, 1975.

————. *A Treatise on Cosmic Fire.* 1925. Reprint. New York: Lucis Publishing Company, 1977.

————. *A Treatise on White Magic.* 1934. Reprint. New York: Lucis Publishing Company, 1974.

Bailey, M. *A Learning Experience.* New York: Lucis Publishing Company, 1990.

Baker, D. *Esoteric Healing,* part I. High Road, Essendon, Herts., England: Dr. Douglas Baker, 1975.

Bernbaum, E. *The Way to Shambhala.* 1980. Reprint. Los Angeles: Jeremy P. Tarcher, 1989.

Blavatsky, H. P. *The Secret Doctrine.* 1888. Reprint. Pasadena, CA: Theosophical University Press, 1977.

Chase, P. L. and Pawlik, J. *The Newcastle Guide to Healing with Gemstones.* North Hollywood, CA: Newcastle Publishing Company, 1989.

Clayman, C. B., ed. *The American Medical Association Encyclopedia of Medicine.* New York: Random House, 1989.

A Course in Miracles. Tiburon, CA: Foundation for Inner Peace, 1975.

The Dimensions of Healing: A Symposium. Los Altos, CA: The Academy of Parapsychology and Medicine, 1972.

Ellenberger, H. F. *The Discovery of the Unconscious.* New York: Basic Books, 1970.

Epstein, G. *Healing Visualizations: Creating Health with Imagery.* New York: Bantam Books, 1989.

Evans-Wentz, W. Y. *The Tibetan Book of the Dead.* Third Edition. New York: Oxford University Press, 1957.

Hall, M. P. *The Therapeutic Value of Music Including the Philosophy of Music.* Los Angeles: The Philosophical Research Society, 1982.

Hilton, J. *Lost Horizon.* 1933. Reprint. New York: Pocket Books, 1990.

Hodson, G. *The Seven Human Temperaments.* 1952. Reprint. Adyar, India: Theosophical Publishing House, 1981.

Johnston, C. *The Yoga Sutras of Patanjali.* 1949. Reprint. London: Stuart & Watkins, 1968.

Kant, I. *Ethical Philosophy.* 1785. Reprint. Indianapolis, IN: Hackett Publishing Company, 1988.

Lansdowne, Z. F. *The Chakras and Esoteric Healing.* York Beach, ME: Samuel Weiser, 1986.

———. *The Rays and Esoteric Psychology.* York Beach, ME: Samuel Weiser, 1989.

———. *Rules for Spiritual Initiation.* York Beach, ME: Samuel Weiser, 1990.

Leadbeater, C. W. *The Chakras.* 1927. Reprint. Wheaton, IL: Theosophical Publishing House, 1977.

———. *The Science of the Sacraments.* Adyar, Madras, India: Theosophical Publishing House, 1920.

Lillard, P. P. *Montessori: A Modern Approach.* New York: Schocken Books, 1972.

McClellan, R. *The Healing Forces of Music.* Amity, NY: Amity House, 1988.

Milewski, J. V. and Harford, J. V. *The Crystal Sourcebook.* Santa Fe, NM: Mystic Crystal Publications, 1988.

Montessori, M. *The Absorbent Mind.* 1949. Reprint. New York: Dell, 1984.

———. *The Advanced Montessori Method,* vol. 1. 1916. Reprint. New York: Schocken Books, 1965.

———. *The Montessori Method.* 1909. Reprint. New York: Schocken Books, 1964.

———. *Reconstruction in Education.* 1948. Reprint. Wheaton, IL: Theosophical Press, 1964.

———. *What You Should Know About Your Child.* 1948. Reprint. Madras, India: Kalakshetra Publications, 1961.

Nikhilananda, Swami. *The Bhagavad Gita.* 1944. Reprint. New York: Ramakrishna-Vivekananda Center, 1969.

Ouseley, S. G. J. *The Power of the Rays.* 1951. Reprint. Essex, England: L. N. Fowler, 1986.

Ramacharaka, Yogi. *The Science of Psychic Healing.* 1909. Reprint. Chicago: Yogi Publication Society, 1937.

Richardson, W. and Huett, L. *Spiritual Value of Gem Stones.* Marina del Rey, CA: DeVorss, 1980.

Robbins, M. D. *Tapestry of the Gods.* Jersey City Heights, NJ: University of the Seven Rays Publishing House, 1988.

Rogers, C. R. *On Becoming A Person*. Boston: Houghton Mifflin, 1961.

Schumann, W. *Gemstones of the World*. 1977. Reprint. New York: Sterling, 1986.

Ullman, D. *Homeopathy: Medicine for the 21st Century*. Berkeley, CA: North Atlantic Books, 1988.

Vithoulkas, G. *The Science of Homeopathy*. New York: Grove Press, 1980.

Weiner, M. and Goss, K. *The Complete Book of Homeopathy*. Garden City, NY: Avery Publishing Group, 1989.

White, J., and S. Krippner, eds. *Future Science*. Garden City, NY: Anchor-Doubleday, 1977.

Wood, E. *The Seven Rays*. 1925. Reprint. Wheaton, IL: Theosophical Publishing House, 1984.

INDEX

Zachary Lansdowne holds a Masters degree in engineering from the Massachusetts Institute of Technology, a Masters degree in philosophy and religion from the California Institute of Integral Studies, a Masters degree in clinical psychology from Antioch University, and a Ph.D. in engineering from Stanford University. In addition to this new work, he is the author of *The Chakras and Esoteric Healing, The Rays and Esoteric Psychology,* and *Rules for Spiritual Initiation,* all published by Samuel Weiser. Lansdowne currently lives in Massachusetts where he is employed as a public policy analyst. He maintains an active interest in counseling and healing work, and lectures all over the United States.